Climate Change, Environments of Uncertainty and Loss

Focusing on one of the most significant and critical issues facing the world today, this important book explores multiple aspects of climate change through the use of Jungian symbols and "signs" of this environmental shift, while diving deep into the politics of loss in reaction to climate chaos, uncertainty, and ambiguity.

Despite the imminent threat of ecological crisis, many treat this existential crisis as something that can be pushed to the side, ignored, and denied. The loss of natural habitats, species, land, human life, and health continues, acknowledged or not. Unconsciously, a necessary process of grief is bubbling up from the depths as a reaction to this climate crisis. This grief, often disguised as anger or inaction, can lead to individual and political action if it is engaged consciously and directed with purpose. From forest fires, to melting ice, to bleached coral, and warming oceans, within the chapters of this book, each sign of our changing planet is explored in depth from multiple perspectives. Through this exploration, each is revealed as a Jungian symbol encompassing so much more than we consciously comprehend. Each symbol is brought to life in the context of this political, communal, and individual space of loss, transforming a subversive grieving process into creative, conscious action.

This is essential and accessible reading for those within the fields of depth psychology, environmental sciences, humanities, and politics, as well as anyone wishing to gain more insight into the current climate crisis and their place within it.

Sarah D. Norton, PhD, is an independent scholar who earned her MA and PhD in Depth Psychology, with an emphasis on Jungian and archetypal psychology at Pacifica Graduate Institute. With a passion for intersectional environmentalism, dreamwork, and creativity, she writes about climate and current events from an archetypal perspective, with a focus on grief, loss, uncertainty, and the novel hope it takes to walk a complex path toward our unknown future.

Routledge Focus on Jung, Politics and Culture

The Jung, Politics and Culture series showcases the 'political turn' in Jungian and Post-Jungian psychology. Established and emerging authors offer unique perspectives and new insights as they explore the connections between Jungian psychology and key topics - including national and international politics, gender, race and human rights.

Titles in the series:

Torture Survivors in Analytical Therapy
Jung, Politics and Culture
Monica Luci

Anti-Semitism and Analytical Psychology
Jung, Politics and Culture
Daniel Burston

A Depth Psychological Study of the Peace Symbol
Jung, Politics and Culture
Michelle Rivera-Clonch

Racial Legacies
Jung, Politics and Culture
Fanny Brewster & Helen Morgan

Torture Survivors in Analytic Therapy
Jung, Politics, Culture
Monica Luci

Climate Change, Environments of Uncertainty and Loss
Jung, Politics and Culture
Sarah D. Norton

For a full list of titles in this series, please visit https://www.routledge.com/Focus-on-Jung-Politics-and-Culture/book-series/FJPC

"Sarah D. Norton's powerful book takes the whole psyche into the existential crisis of the twenty-first century: the climate catastrophe. By exposing rise of political rage as rooted in unconscious loss and grief, the book provides a map of terrain that we must traverse. For without the exploration of the psychic legacies of colonialism, speciesism, and inequality provided here, real transformation is stuck. Perhaps not surprisingly, Norton shows C. G. Jung as prescient and helpful in unsticking the wheels of change. This book is desperately needed to tell the story of where we are and how to foster necessary forgiveness and hope."

Susan Rowland (*PhD*), *Pacifica Graduate Institute, author with Joel Weishaus of* Jungian Arts-Based Research and the Nuclear Enchantment of New Mexico (*2021*)

"This creative and transdisciplinary addition to the *Jung, Politics and Culture* series engages with core depth issues concerning the climate crisis. Norton explores the unconscious tendrils of grief that entangle so many people in a stifling sense of doom. From mythology and folktales to economics and activism, we experience a hopeful text that takes an enlivening post-Jungian approach to the imagery, symbolism, psychology, and politics of climate change."

Andrew Samuels, *Author of* The Political Psyche

"Sarah D. Norton masterfully weaves depth psychology, political analysis, and environmental science together to explore the complex emotional and societal impacts of our climate crisis. With profound insight and compassion, Norton's transdisciplinary approach offers a unique and vital perspective on one of the most pressing issues of our time. This book is an essential read for anyone seeking to understand and navigate the psychological and universal dimensions of climate change."

Roula-Maria Dib (*PhD*), *Director, London Arts-Based Research Center, Founding Editor, Indelible, author of* Jungian Metaphor in Modernist Literature (*2020*), *and poet,* Simply Being (*2021*)

"Sarah D. Norton's powerful book takes the whole psyche into the existential crisis of the twenty-first century: the climate catastrophe. By exposing rise of political rage as rooted in unconscious loss and grief, the book provides a map of terrain that we must traverse. For without the exploration of the psychic legacies of colonialism, speciesism, and inequality provided here, real transformation is stuck. Perhaps not surprisingly, Norton shows C. G. Jung as prescient and helpful in unsticking the wheels of change. This book is desperately needed to tell the story of where we are and how to foster necessary forgiveness and hope."

Susan Rowland (*PhD*), *Pacifica Graduate Institute, author with Joel Weishaus of* Jungian Arts-Based Research and the Nuclear Enchantment of New Mexico (*2021*)

"This creative and transdisciplinary addition to the *Jung, Politics and Culture* series engages with core depth issues concerning the climate crisis. Norton explores the unconscious tendrils of grief that entangle so many people in a stifling sense of doom. From mythology and folktales to economics and activism, we experience a hopeful text that takes an enlivening post-Jungian approach to the imagery, symbolism, psychology, and politics of climate change."

Andrew Samuels, *Author of* The Political Psyche

"Sarah D. Norton masterfully weaves depth psychology, political analysis, and environmental science together to explore the complex emotional and societal impacts of our climate crisis. With profound insight and compassion, Norton's transdisciplinary approach offers a unique and vital perspective on one of the most pressing issues of our time. This book is an essential read for anyone seeking to understand and navigate the psychological and universal dimensions of climate change."

Roula-Maria Dib (*PhD*), *Director, London Arts-Based Research Center, Founding Editor, Indelible, author of* Jungian Metaphor in Modernist Literature (*2020*), *and poet,* Simply Being (*2021*)

Climate Change, Environments of Uncertainty and Loss

Jung, Politics and Culture

Sarah D. Norton

LONDON AND NEW YORK

First published 2025
by Routledge
4 Park Square, Milton Park, Abingdon, Oxon OX14 4RN

and by Routledge
605 Third Avenue, New York, NY 10158

Routledge is an imprint of the Taylor & Francis Group, an informa business

British Library Cataloguing-in-Publication Data
A catalogue record for this book is available from the British Library

ISBN: 978-1-032-64481-3 (hbk)
ISBN: 978-1-032-64483-7 (pbk)
ISBN: 978-1-032-64482-0 (ebk)

DOI: 10.4324/9781032644820

Typeset in Times New Roman
by codeMantra

Dedicated to Mammy, my grandmother, who passed before she could read these pages and yet whose love of this world and compassion for others shaped every word.

Contents

Figures

Acknowledgments

I would like to express my deep appreciation to a number of people in the process through which this book came to fruition. First is to Andrew Samuels for putting out a call through the International Association for Jungian Studies (IAJS) list serve. His generosity and interest in expanding the work of Jungian psychology to independent scholars like me is commendable. To the IAJS and the Jungian Society of Scholarly Studies (JSSS) for the same inclusive nature and connections for students and scholars alike. Presenting at conferences for IAJS and the London Arts Based Research Center (LABRC) helped me immensely over the past few years to connect to others and expand ideas within my field and beyond, a true gift in these pandemic times. To Pacifica Graduate Institute, where I gained my PhD in Depth Psychology with an emphasis on Jungian and Archetypal Studies, but especially to my dissertation chair, professor there, and friend, Susan Rowland, who has always been a champion of my work and encouraged me to take these ideas out into the world.

To the editorial staff at Routledge, especially Katie Randall, for her support and patience as I navigated the process toward publication.

On a more personal note, I'd like to thank my parents for their encouragement and love in everything that I do. To my husband for his patience and support as I find my way through the various roles of caregiver, writer, partner, editor, and more. To my colleagues and our founder at The Foundation for Family and Community Healing (FFCH) in Richmond, VA, thank you for the time and space to juggle personal projects while serving our community through the FFCH mission and vision.

And lastly, to all those struggling in our world with loss, grief, uncertainty, ambiguity, and the unknown. I hope the following pages honor this space we find ourselves in, hold it with love, and can be a supportive companion into whatever lies ahead.

Introduction

Climates of Uncertainty, Ambiguity, and Loss

At the very end of his closing chapter in the first book of this *Jung, Politics and Culture* series, Thomas Singer wrote that in the face of what he termed "extinction anxiety," as it sounds its alarm all around us,

> our response needs to come from the whole of the psyche in harnessing all our political, psychological, and spiritual efforts to forge a unity of deep action on behalf of creation and against that which would destroy it. This may well require the extinction of our current worldview, which is focused almost exclusively on materialist reductionisms of all kinds.
>
> (p. 150)

This is the thread I believe this book is picking up, the banner it is carrying forward from the start of this incredible series. Not only do we need "deep action on behalf of creation," but we also need creativity toward deep action. We need sacrifice and acknowledgment of the grief that spirals around hope. We need to step into a space of loss to reconstitute a new path forward. For, without loss or the possibility of it, there is no transformation or necessary discomfort to spur change. In the spirit of facing that loss head on, I'd like to take some time to set the stage, not only for the following chapters, but to give those less familiar with the landscape of climate policy a brief, but hopefully thorough enough primer as to where we stand in this day and age. By understanding the underpinnings of our current situation, the images later on will have more of a grounded voice.

One of the biggest political topics in our world today is climate change, at least it should be, and I believe, for a growing number of people, it is. Whether you follow the science or rail against it, things are changing and we have to figure out a way forward in the face of uncertainty. With the 2022 Intergovernmental Panel on Climate Change (IPCC) report coming in and COP28 (28th Council of the Parties to the United Nations (UN) Framework Convention on Climate Change Conference (UNFCCC)) in December 2023, we are facing a politically charged moment for the environment on a global scale. Every day we continue our current trajectory it becomes even

DOI: 10.4324/9781032644820-1

more politically immediate and impactful. Despite the imminent threat of this ecological crisis, we treat it as a distant existential threat. Existential here being referenced tongue and cheek in the sense of an existential crisis influencers warn about on TikTok wherein they mean something that seems to cause a moment of deep concern but is easily dismissed and pushed aside for the viral video of the day and forgotten. Rather, the immediacy of the crisis we face is existential in the root meaning of the word, something that speaks to our very existence as a species, one of life and loss.

Sadly, in the years since the Paris Accord (2015) at COP21, things have only gotten more dire and now the need to change our current ways can no longer be pushed aside or ignored. In truth, it should have been a much more striking concern decades ago, but we are far behind the curve. Nevertheless, many individuals and nations continue to push climate into the shadows. This is even more concerning as we come to terms with the inequity of this global crisis. At the latest Council of the Parties, COP28, held in Dubai, the tension of this gap in understanding was evident from the start. Months before the conference began, there was already great concern over the choice of host. The United Arab Emirates (UAE) is a leading figure in the fossil fuel market, it was hard for those concerned to imagine that a host country with that kind of investment in oil could champion the kind of movement needed to center climate concerns (Batrawy, 2023).

Furthermore, the UAE chose Sultan al-Jaber to preside over COP28. He is the chairman of a state-backed renewable energy company, but he is also the chief executive of a state-owned oil company (Batrawy, 2023). As the COP grew closer, the list of attendees and delegates began to trickle out. By the time COP28 started, the largest delegation was, as expected for a host country, the UAE. This was followed by Brazil (who is scheduled to host the next major conference, COP30 in 2025) and the third largest number of attendees were the fossil fuel lobbyists, numbering, at last count 2,456, "nearly 4 times as many as last year" (Democracy Now!, 2023) and more than any other non-host delegation. Not only that, but they far outnumbered the 1,509 delegates from the "ten most climate vulnerable nations" and "more than seven times the number … [of] official indigenous representatives (316)" (Kick Big Polluters Out, 2023).

By the end of COP28 there were mixed reviews on the path forward. There were some big steps, a consensus was reached by all parties on a path forward. One which numerous delegates stated was to keep us on track to 1.5°C, "our North Star." For anyone not as steeped in the climate conversation, this 1.5°C marker is a goal that was set out in the Paris Agreement from COP21 in 2015 (UNFCCC, 2015). This marker refers to the most ambitious goal set out at that COP, one that would keep the global average temperature within 1.5°C above the pre-industrial baseline from 1850 to 1900 (World Meteorological Organization, 2023). This agreement has long been a point of contention within environmentally minded circles. Many saw it, especially as the years moved on, as a failure. Though there was an agreement made by all parties, very few were on track to meet the goals set forward there and there were little to no repercussions policy-wise to get them back on track.

To call this the North Star for climate policy and direction is an interesting and important choice of terminology. The North Star is also called Polaris or the Pole Star, noting the polar nature of it in line with Earth's axis. In navigation, it is a point which is considered constant, never moving. No matter where one finds oneself, if they can pinpoint the North Star they can navigate from there. In many Indigenous cultures of Turtle Island (North America), the North Star is referred to as *Ti-yn-sōu-dă-go-êrr* ("Star that Never Moves," Iroquois), *Kái yicíŋ·adi pá·tusuba* ("Not Moving Star," Northern Paiute), and a number of other names including the Algonquian speaking Blackfoot name "Star that Stands Still" (Miller, 1997, pp. 47, 129, 264). There is a constant to all of these, even the creation stories around them note their permanence and steadfastness. In times of uncertainty, a guiding, constant star is of utmost importance and can give a sense of direction to even the most circuitous journey. It can also serve as an example of waiting, a symbol guiding us to find moments of calm in the chaos swirling around us.

One of the points from Paris was followed up at COP26 hosted in Glasgow (2021). This was putting in place an "ambition mechanism" to "assess collective progress towards achieving its purpose and long-term goals" (UNFCCC, 2023). This mechanism was referred to as the Global Stocktake (GST) and the first one was published and gaveled into an agreement at COP28 with one to follow every five years. This GST was a guiding factor at COP28 and seems to have been a major motivation behind much in the final text. However, as US representative and US Special Presidential Envoy for Climate John Kerry said in his closing remarks at the final plenary "nobody here will see their complete views reflected" (December 13, 2023, 1hr 35min). This is somewhat true, but it is perhaps more accurate to say, by the statements made by many countries at the same closing session, that the concerns of smaller, developing countries and delegations, many on the front lines of climate issues, were most poorly reflected. There was a great gap in the text, the procedures, and the needed guidance on policy going forward.

Given this lacuna, this gap, this book digs into this politics of loss. Not only the more obvious loss of natural habitats, species, health, land, and human life that we are confronted with in the ongoing climate crisis. But also, the loss we need to undertake to move forward and the recognition of grieving that is already happening on an unconscious level. This necessary process of grief is already bubbling up from the depths as a reaction to climate chaos. As is so often the case with grief, it is cleverly disguised as anger, anxiety, denial, or emotional paralysis when unacknowledged. If we dig deeply within ourselves and our societies, we will find it there. In this place of loss, this unconscious or underground space, specific images commonly associated as "signs" of this environmental chaos become a guiding star.

Throughout the following pages each image is opened and explored deeply, chapter by chapter, moving the image from a sign of global warming to a Jungian symbol. Each one can then find its place within the context of this political, communal, and individual space of loss. In this way, the images transform this subversive grieving process forward into conscious action. From chapter to chapter, image by image, we will explore the idea of Global Warming as a hyperobject (from the work of Timothy Morton, 2013), the politics of loss and grief, specifically ambiguous loss from the work of Pauline Boss (1999, 2006, 2021), and some passages from Jung's *Black Books* (2020) to illuminate the deeper patterns at work in the archetypal layers of this political issue.

I will also note here that the majority of passages quoted from the *Black Books* below have been chosen not only because they were surprisingly fitting to the themes despite being written over a century ago, but because they are passages that were lost in translation. They are ones which series editor Sonu Shamdasani, in his impressive notations between volumes, mentions were not included in the subsequent *Red Book: Liber Novus* (2009a). The *Red Book* had popular appeal due to its size, illustrations, and general intrigue, there was even a reader's edition published (2009b). Given the popularity and cost of the original, these missing passages fall into the area of loss. Many will not have read these or are slowly still making their way through the seven volumes. I was intent on finding what was left behind, knowing that even though they were not included consciously in the *Red Book*, they were sitting silently below the surface. This is just to say that loss comes in many forms and is explored throughout as things can be lost in translation, lost in moving a dream experience into conscious language, and when confronting the literal loss of ecosystems and loved ones.

Even more important on the political side of this topic is the loss that we need to undertake to move forward in a changing world. A willing sacrifice must be made to move into a space of renewed hope, one that does not cling to the past, but looks toward the future. This loss, in our current political climate, is so often framed as a loss of freedom. However, using each image, we will gain a new perspective, viewing the "loss" instead as a necessary sacrifice for the collective that is best undertaken by conscious choice than being thrust upon us unconsciously. Moving our collective action into the realm of the sacred and exploring further, we will begin to understand that this is a both/and world. These moves need to be undertaken not only on an individual level, but in our local, national, and worldwide communities.

One of the greatest disappointments at COP28, was the loss of strong language. There had been rumors floating about that this may be *the* COP to finally put the brakes on fossil fuels. Many protest groups had signs and slogans inside and around the world in early December touting "Fast, Fair, Funded, Phase Out." (In a handful of these chants we also heard the term feminist as the fifth "F" in this slogan one that seems important to acknowledge those who are often discarded and left out of these discussions, a blanket term for those who are marginalized.) There was a lot of debate and reaction to the choice of the term "phase-down" instead (Carrington, 2023). The science is clear, in the IPCC, the GST, and the WMO report just prior to COP28, humans are contributing to climate change and the burning of fossil fuels is the overwhelming cause. We have to half emissions by 2050 to have any hope of landing near the 1.5 target. This was emphasized over and over throughout COP28, remember that "North Star"? To place the goal of "phasing out" fossil fuels gives a much more marked directive, they need to be reduced to almost zero. Phasing down "is a weaker term, indicating … [a] decline without specifying by how much or when" (Carrington, 2023).

Almost all the data coming in from this past year and looking ahead to 2025 suggests that we have already overshot our North Star. Yet, there is still time to keep us away from 2°C where we will face an even more difficult and uncertain future. However, we cannot get there by simply "phasing down" fossil fuel use or reaching "Net Zero" emissions. "Net zero" means that we are sequestering as much carbon as we are putting into the atmosphere. In our current climate emergency, with the possibility of intensifying feedback loops that are already in place (for example, melting permafrost releasing trapped methane), net zero is not nearly enough. These natural carbon contributors are rarely factored into many corporate or policy models. Maybe, if we were to completely eliminate fossil fuel use, we could have a fighting chance to zero out contributions from humans. However, new or existing systems to sequester carbon are faltering and existing carbon sinks are being pushed to their limits. At this point we have to go farther, phasing down will not suffice. These omissions in the language are a huge loss, so much intent, direction, and accountability could be brought forward by stronger and more targeted language.

Ironically, this loss of language is due to the loss avoidance of certain sectors which are invested in the use of fossil fuels—oil, coal, and gas. As indicated earlier, these sectors were heavily represented in the COP28 climate negotiations. On one level, to have the phase down of fossil fuels is a great victory, one that was much touted in those closing statements, especially by Western, high-income countries. For much of the rest of the world, this meager use of phase down rather than phase out can be the point of loss that makes all the difference. Yes, COP28 set ambitious goals to triple renewable energy and double energy efficiency by 2030, they even set goals to halt and reverse deforestation and reduce CO_2 emissions and greenhouse gas (GHG, which importantly includes methane). COP28 even began with some of the most ambitious loss and damage plans. These intend to lay out financial and technological help for low-income countries being funded by high-income countries, something that has been needed for many years.

Honestly, if you have been paying attention, none of this is new. Most of these goals were in the Paris Agreement, at least sketches of what they needed to become. This is the problem of loss we still face in policy and that so many delegates from COP28 railed about in statements and protests scattered throughout. It is one thing to know about an issue, it is quite another to move forward to address it in an equitable and just manner for all involved. The citizens of low-lying island countries throughout the world, but most specifically at COP28, from the Pacific Island nations, many of whom were represented by indigenous voices, are already feeling the pressure of climate change.

Sea levels are already becoming untenable where they live. In Africa and many of the countries in Asia the heat of the summer is increasingly unbearable and deadly. Without the infrastructure some higher income nations have, death and loss are inevitable already. Within high-income countries as well, the problem of inequality within one country is a life and loss issue: homes taken by extreme weather, deaths from heat or cold without means to supplement failing infrastructure, communities of color forced to confront terrible pollution of air, water, and soil, and indigenous voices that are overlooked, arrested, or vilified for speaking out for our shared resources, land, and water. When we look to the future, we must look for a way forward that brings those who are most at risk and those who are impacted disproportionately to the fore—the way forward must be a fast, fair, funded, feminist, phase-out.

In other words, we need a perspective of complexity and diversity when facing the uncertainty of our climate future. Though I am a middle-income white woman from the United States of America, I hope to serve as an ally to many communities and global voices throughout the following chapters. Climate change, climate crisis, global warming, climate chaos, the climate emergency, “the global boiling” as UN Secretary General Antonio Guterres said in July 2023 (UN News), whatever you term it, it is a worldwide issue that cannot be relegated to one place or another. That being said, one cannot realistically include every marginalized or disaffected group, so I have chosen those voices which serve the images most poignantly in the following pages.

By focusing on the image we can get down to the Jungian level of this *Jung, Politics and Culture* series. In Jung’s psychology of the unconscious, the images from dreams, mythology, folktales, even those in cultural productions like film, literature, and television have an archetypal aspect to them, they are symbols of something more. They have an energetic core that connects each of us to that emotional root. This level is known to us but can never be fully known, there will always be an air of mystery, something that connects us to the unconscious and a level of a certain loss that leads not to melancholy but, rather, to wonder.

In the last chapter of the first book of this series, *Vision, Reality and Complex: Jung, Politics and Culture* by Thomas Singer (2021), the concept of “extinction anxiety” (p. 144) is named. Singer further states that, unlike the one other use he could find, he is referring to “the fear of extinction” (2021) and that this is “where the spirit of the times and the spirit of the depths meet” (2021, p. 146). As I read that I recognized my call to this work. To be anxious about extinction is ultimately an anxiety of loss, a place of grieving, and a platform on which we must state our grievances, however small they may seem. From the images in the following chapters, wildfires, melting ice, bleached coral, pollution, and rising oceans. We will encounter the politics of loss, from the tiniest coral polyp to the vast ice sheets at the poles of our planet. Each one will drag us into the spirit of the depths and have us soaring with the spirit of the times.

Further down in that same chapter "Extinction Anxiety: Where the spirit of the depths meets the spirit of the times, or extinction anxiety and the yearning for annihilation" (pp. 143–151). Singer references the Doomsday Clock (p. 148). This metric, set forward by the Bulletin of Atomic Scientists in 1947, is now (as of January 23, 2024) set to 90 seconds before midnight "the closest to global catastrophe it has ever been" they state on their website. A full minute closer than when Singer was writing about it a few short years ago. This is "the closest to global catastrophe it has ever been" (Mecklin, 2024). This imaginary space on an amorphous countdown clock places us, as a global society, within a locus of severe uncertainty and ambiguity. This is a place of loss that has been, is happening, and, at the same time, has not happened yet.

It is the uncertainty of this that can become a place of wonder, the ambiguity, the terrible beauty of that space that I hope we can all walk through together in the following chapters. Whether you come from a Jungian academic background, like mine, or not, the intention of following these images is to keep us always rooted in the wonder of this issue and wondering about the issue of climate. Politics and culture are passions of mine, which is why taking this project on was such an exciting challenge. Though I am not a political scientist, I am what some might term a political nerd. I watch almost all the debates, of both parties, I have rarely missed voting in an election, no matter how small (aka. local), and I probably do a little too much doomscrolling (if you don't know this term, we will explore it shortly). Overall, the main impetus for bringing all these layers of knowledge together is my passion for our planet and all the people who coexist upon this earth.

In addition to honoring the diversity of our global culture, my intention is to make this addition to the series a transdisciplinary endeavor. Transdisciplinarity, as theorized by Basarab Nicolescu (2005), is extremely fitting for this endeavor which seeks to hold uncertainty and not knowing. In his theory, "knowledge is neither exterior or interior: it is simultaneously exterior and interior" (p. 8); it is both/and, something that will be found throughout the following text. This is a place where uncertainty and both/and-ness have to be confronted and held. To go beyond disciplines, or perhaps into the depths of disciplines, I hope to embark upon an inquiry into the subjects of climate change from a new angle. "Transdisciplinarity recognizes we are living in a complex, uncertain, and pluralistic world" (Montuori, 2006/2008). This type of inquiry requires one to be fully in the world, interacting with the subjects, creating relationships with them. From images to nature, to dreams, to economic and political theories and policies, relationships will be created here. As I dive into each of these, as you read these musings, the greatest achievement of this work will be that it brings you into a relationship with these as well.

I will be pulling from my own field of Jungian and archetypal psychology, from political science, literary studies, economics, environmental science, and more. No matter what brought you here, I hope you will find a place for your passion within these pages. One that spurs you forward in this uncertain time to create a new, complex, and diverse vision of what our future can look like. The main gift of not knowing is that the outcome can be anything we imagine. The science may be clear, but how we go into the next few decades can make a massive difference, especially to the quality of life we can have as global citizens. Perhaps we can surprise ourselves! So, I invite you to step forward with me now, into this place of anxiety, uncertainty, loss, and the known, not with a view to despair, but to step into a new way forward, eyes open, heart soft, creativity and imagination at the ready, into wonder and possibility.

Resources

Batrawy, A. (2023, December 9). What it means for an oil producing country, the UAE, to host U.N. climate talks. *National Public Radio: Climate.* https://www.npr.org/2023/12/09/1217970348/what-it-means-for-an-oil-producing-country-the-uae-to-host-un-climate-talks

Boss, P. (1999). *Ambiguous loss: learning to live with unresolved grief.* Harvard University Press.

Boss, P. (2006). *Loss, trauma, and resilience: Therapeutic work with ambiguous loss.* W.W. Norton and Company.

Boss, P. (2021). *The myth of closure: Ambiguous loss in a time of pandemic and change.* W.W. Norton and Company.

Carrington, D. (2023, December 9). Why is the phase-out of fossil fuels the biggest flashpoint at Cop28? *The Guardian.* https://www.theguardian.com/environment/2023/dec/09/phase-out-down-fossil-fuels-cop28

Jung, C. G. (2020). *The black books: 1913–1932 notebooks of transformation, Vols 1–7.* (In S.Shamdasani, Ed.). (M. Liebscer, J. Peck, S. Shamdasani, Trans.). W.W. Norton and Company.

Jung, C. G., & Shamdasani, S. (2009a). *The red book: Liber* novus (S. Shamdasani, Ed.). Norton.

Jung, C. G., & Shamdasani, S. (2009b). *The red book: Liber* novus (Readers ed.). (S. Shamdasani, Ed.). Norton.

Kick Big Polluters Out, London. (2023, December 5). *Record number of fossil fuel lobbyists at COP28* [Press Release]. https://kickbigpollutersout.org/articles/release-record-number-fossil-fuel-lobbyists-attend-cop28

Mecklin, J. (Ed.). (2024, January 23). *2024 doomsday clock announcement.* Bulletin of the Atomic Scientists. https://thebulletin.org/doomsday-clock/current-time/

Montuori, A. (2008). Forward: Transdisciplinarity. In B. Nicolescu (Ed.), *Transdisciplinarity theory and practice.* Hampton Press. (Original work 2006.)

Morton, T. (2013). *Hyperobjects: Philosophy and ecology after the end of the world.* University of Minnesota Press.

Nicolescu, B. (2005, September 6–12). *Transdisciplinarity-Past, present and future* [Lecture]. Second Congress of Transdisciplinarity, Villa Velha, Brazil. https://www.tercercongresomundialtransdisciplinariedad.mx/wp-content/uploads/2019/08/Transdisciplinarity-past-present-and-future.pdf

Planet for sale? Record 2,500 fossil fuel lobbyists descend on COP28 U.N. climate summit in Dubai. (2023, December 5). Democracy Now! https://www.democracynow.org/2023/12/5/record_number_of_lobbyists_at_cop28

Singer, T. (2021). *Vision, reality and complex: Jung, politics and culture* (Focus on Jung, Politics and Culture). Routledge.

UNFCCC. (2023, December 13). *Closing plenary: 6th meeting of CMP and CMA* [Video]. United Nations Climate Change. https://unfccc.int/event/6th-meeting-of-the-cop-6th-meeting-of-the-cmp-6th-meeting-of-the-cma

United Nations Framework Convention on Climate Change (UNFCCC) (2015). *The Paris agreement.* https://unfccc.int/process-and-meetings/the-paris-agreement

UN News (2023, July 27). Hottest July ever signals 'era of global boiling has arrived' says UN chief. *UN news.* https://news.un.org/en/story/2023/07/1139162

World Meteorological Organization (2023). *Provisional state of the global climate in 2023.* https://wmo.int/sites/default/files/2023-11/WMO%20Provisional%20State%20of%20the%20Global%20Climate%202023.pdf

1 Navigating Doom into an Uncertain Future

This feeling of extinction, of doomsday is all around us, in film and television shows set in an apocalyptic future, with terms like doomscrolling so ubiquitous it was a Merriam-Webster "word we are watching" in 2020 and, as of September 2023, has been added to their official listings. When they were watching the term, they stated "during times of crisis and uncertainty, some of us pay more attention to the news, looking for answers … when you can't stop scrolling … or reading news that you know will make you sad, anxious, or angry" you are doomscrolling. This is now essentially the official definition of the term. If you've spent any time on social media, you have probably noticed the snarky "Ok, doomer" memes and trolling comments making the rounds, especially in the areas of climate conversation. Given the vast nature of this issue and the uncertainty that surrounds it, doom is in the air.

Doom today commonly denotes darkness, evil, and a sense of the end times. There is a feel of post-apocalyptic, sepia-toned landscapes, and growling, clicking zombies just around the bend. Underneath this, if we look back further into its etymology one will find that it has a somewhat innocuous start. In old English, the term dōm referred to a statute or judgment. It is of Germanic origin from a base meaning "to put in place" related to "do." This eventually evolved in middle English to doome and brought with it a feeling of laying down judgment as with Domr in Old Norse (Harper, 2024). Eventually, this judgment came to connote the idea of condemning someone: to their fate, to death, or otherwise. Slowly doom crept into the realm of doomsdays, apocalyptic fantasy, and now, doomscrolling. "'You have no means to judge the value of present things in any way; that only manifests itself later, if things are of value at all. One needs to live with uncertainty. That is for certain …'" (Jung, 2020, p. 263, v. 4). Interestingly, this passage did not make it into Jung's much lauded, posthumous, and beautifully illustrated *Red Book: Liber Novus* (2009), it was left to fade into obscurity in his personal journals which he kept from 1913 until 1932, finally published posthumously in 2020. Perhaps he was just too uncertain of it and the future it pointed to.

DOI: 10.4324/9781032644820-2

In Jung's time, as a white, Protestant man of a certain European, privileged economic class, this sense of doom seemed to point to the looming threat of World War II. In our time, in terms of climate, we are facing mass extinction, depletion of biodiversity, deforestation, ocean acidification, food and water instability, sea-level rise, ice melt, coral bleaching, various issues of pollution from microplastics to air quality, and so much more. The difficulty of this is the ambiguity and complexity of it all. All these issues are either looming on the horizon, actively affecting front-line communities, or both. They are also not completely irreversible. This is one of the many challenges with climate data, it relies on an array of models. In fact, "uncertainty is at the core of the climate change problem" (Mehta & Srivastava, 2020, p. 99) in that it is difficult to "predict the scale, intensity, and impact … on human and natural environments." The second half of this statement is attributed to Curry and Webster (2011) in "Climate Science and the Uncertainty Monster." We will dive into their analysis a bit later, for our current track, suffice it to say, uncertainty is daunting, hence the monstrous title.

When confronted with the level of unpredictability that climate data brings or with the everyday ambiguities around what the future may bring, we get a sense that something is missing, there is a loss or lack. This missing piece is a relevant source of data that science cannot measure currently, the upcoming weather patterns that only make sense after the season, or the sea ice levels that cannot officially be recognized as outliers until the yearly rates are tolled, all of this is felt as a loss. It's a unique loss of something in between, we may still have it, but at the same time it is gone. The major quality of this class of loss, one that is not fully realized, is what Pauline Boss (2006) termed ambiguous, a loss that is both unclear and indeterminate (p. 6). "The uncertainty makes ambiguous loss the most distressful of all losses" (Boss, 2006, p. 6). Once one has experienced this type of loss, even for a brief time, they can understand why. There is a strange hanging on that never let's go, sometimes even long after the initial loss is resolved one way or the other.

In Boss's earlier texts (1999, 2006), ambiguous loss has two main descriptions, either "perceiving loved ones as present when they are physically gone … or perceiving them as gone when they are physically present" (Boss, 2006, p. 7). In the former case, this could be someone who is missing in action, has run away or was taken from their loved ones. In the latter case, most often due to ailments such as Alzheimer's, dementia, or even addiction. Boss goes on to explain that the reason this kind of loss is so insidious is the uncertainty of it all. This kind of loss is extremely hard to grasp, it can leave one frozen with no path forward. There is no community ritualization of the loss, no funeral or formal recognition to be gained, especially for their grief, this can leave one disconnected and misunderstood. Finally, this is a loss that can continue indefinitely, until there is an acknowledged death, an individual or body found, a cure or a release, the loss continues on with "relentless uncertainty" (Boss, 2006, pp. 7–8).

Waiting

I experienced this kind of loss for a distinct seven-week period when my mother fell into a coma after experiencing a brain aneurysm. In truth, the loss continued well past that initial period, even more than a decade out, I still feel the pangs of uncertainty and grief for the mother I knew before. This is the strangest, most surreal experience. In those seven weeks, where she was shuffled from hospital to hospital, hooked up to various machines, and evaluated constantly, there was no response detected. The doctors were baffled, my family was beside themselves, everyone clinging to a hope for something that may never come. Day after day we waited. I performed all the necessary tasks, helping to run the family business, assisting when I could at the medical facilities, sending out updates to friends and family, eating, barely sleeping; on, and on, and on. I cannot imagine what it must be like for those whose loved ones are struggling with long-term illness or who have been missing for years or decades. Eventually the doctors handling my mother's case decided to try a last-ditch surgery. Almost miraculously, for what is magic other than science we don't yet understand, she was awake and responsive! After seven weeks in a coma and significant injury within her brain, she was different. Because of all we had been through I was different too and our relationship was forever changed.

The time of ambiguity while she was in the coma was the most acute. I wish I had found Boss's writing around then. Unfortunately, I did not discover it until years later. Even so, I knew there was something unique about this time of loss, uncertainty, and ambiguity. I could never express it aloud. I would talk to people during the seven weeks who were generally optimistic and hopeful around me, those who weren't, I sometimes appreciated more. I wanted to rail and cry and grieve, to share this loss with others, but no one was there. Honestly, I was afraid to let myself feel that uncertainty completely. I kept busy. That was my antidote. This is a valid coping mechanism, but it cannot last forever, at some point things have to come to a head.

For me, it took quite a while and a bit of separation before I started to confront the uncertainty ahead. As the days went on, she moved from one facility to another. The first hospital where she was treated after her initial assessment became home for a few weeks. During that time, ironically, there was a clock outside her window. It was a sort of clock tower in the hospital courtyard, but it was perpetually stuck around 6:30 with hands pointing up and down at once. What a potent symbol for that time, a clock stuck halfway through the hour, half up, half down both, and a perfect metaphor for that time of ambiguity. We finally moved on from there to a rehab center closer to home, where friends and family could come visit more readily. I was relieved to have others to share the load, to be there by her bedside, but the optimistic reports of her reacting to singing or stories or the like became worse to bear.

It wasn't that I didn't believe she would never wake, I just knew the likelihood of when it happened, her being the mother I remembered would be a distant memory. While others were holding on, I was trying to figure out where we were going given all the possible outcomes. This split future was harder to hold onto. Indeed "the future is dark and everything to come still needs to be done.' The uncertainty and unpredictability are difficult to bear" (Jung in conversation with his soul, 2020, p. 262, vol. 4). This suggestion of an uncertain future, found in Jung's *Black Books* holds this feeling of doom exemplified in that dark future, that presage of his soul. At times, when the future felt like Jung described, I just wished for a solid path forward, even if it was the worst outcome. This is the shadow of uncertainty; all the worst impulses win out. You rale and cry and scream and bargain, you deny and avoid and grieve. In the confrontation with these worst outcomes, I realized anything else would be a gift and one not to be scoffed at. If she woke up, even if no piece of her was left that I recognized or that recognized me, there was still something to build from, to move forward with.

The key here was I had to confront and accept the worst of the possibilities, only then could I begin to imagine a new way forward. This is where I began to come to terms with the parallels of my personal experience with the challenges that face us all today. I could see the path I was on, waiting, not knowing, various unsure futures ahead as a strange echo of the climate crisis. Lucky for me I had a guide through, a strong image connected to the climate emergency (more on this next chapter) as well as a deep rooting in Jungian psychology and dream work to move me through.

Wondering

I am a long-time dream journal keeper. I have pages, journals, and digital notes on my phone full of dreams from over the years. Even though so much of this time had me so wrapped up in waking life, and with interrupted sleep, I only remembered a few dreams. Nevertheless, the pieces and dreams I remembered at that time gave me a strange comfort. Loss of this type, its ambiguity, requires a new kind of grief and a renewed hope to get to the other side, it also requires an acknowledgment of the situation we find ourselves in. "More than scientifically precise answers, metaphors and symbols allow us to transcend the immediate situation and find meaning in our loss" (Boss, 1999, p. 131). Boss mentions this in regard to storytelling by those who are missing loved ones, for me this came in dreams, for others perhaps it is through therapy or activism. To find and tell a new story, or more importantly in the face of climate chaos, to tell as many stories as we can about what the future could look like is key.

Sociologist Peter Marris (1974/2014) wrote that when confronted by a crisis, be it an individual, group, or society as a whole "it provokes a conflict between contradictory impulses—to return to the past, and to forget it altogether" (p. 151). This is where we seem to be on the climate issue, this is where stories can play a role. Rather than pretending that it isn't happening, or that we have years left to figure out a solution or, on the flip side, ignoring the crisis completely, we need to imagine a way forward, to tell new stories. In my mother's case, my dreams were infinitely helpful in this way. In one, I dreamed that my mother was lying on a bed of light, the light was bright and comforting, it felt like pure love. As she lay there, I knew it was everyone who was thinking about her powering that healing light, she did not wake, but I knew she was well. In another, she did wake, but she was like a child, joyous, naïve, and full of potential. In a third, she was up and about, in a wheelchair and somewhat delayed in her responses to everyone, but present and loving. We wheeled through hospital corridors, wondering what would happen next and who we might encounter.

Each of these, in its own way, came to pass and, at the same time, none of them "came true." This is the case with dreams. In my dreams, there was a deeper truth that was coming forward, the "dream come true" scenario, no matter what happened there was a path forward if we held the situation with love and a vision, or light, on the path ahead. Perhaps this is one of the greatest gifts of dreams and imagination, as well as uncertainty. Marris noted that the "confidence in the predictability of our surroundings rests not only on the accident of living—except in dreams—in a consistent world," of course dreams fall outside of a "consistent world," but rather "on our ability to abstract from particular events the underlying laws which govern them" (p. 6). Here he seems to say that there is a sort of conservative politics to our daily life.

We gather information as we go through life, just living life is a sort of consistent democratization of experience. Each encounter or observation adds its input to our lived experience. As life goes on and things stay relatively the same, we can rely on certain things happening a certain way. We become more and more conservative in our mindset. Marris mentions that in a political view "conservatism is an attempt to consolidate established norms of behavior and the principles which justify them … it is a condition of survival" (pp. 7–8). Today, this can be a very literal situation. As the climate becomes more unstable, the things that fall outside of our usual patterns and behaviors can seem especially jarring. The more and more these strange occurrences accumulate, like a snowball rolling downhill, it can quickly accumulate into something we cannot run away from or feel the threat of this crushing weight.

For me, the dreams allowed me to let go of some of those conservative impulses. Imagining new routines, new relationships, and finding whatever gifts might lie within became an important practice. Whenever I woke with a dream I used it as an opening, maybe not always in that moment or on that day, but I let the images live in my imagination to see where they would lead in the weeks and months that followed. As the doomsday clock ticks closer to midnight this liminal space of uncertainty can become fertile ground for connection and understanding. If we can see our way through, embracing the looming darkness, this uncertainty can become a guiding light toward change.

Wandering

I had a dream quite a number of years ago where I was in a wood paneled room, quite dark. It had the feeling of an underground storehouse or something like a deckhand's quarters on an old pirate ship. As my eyes grew accustomed to the darkness, I noticed a table and a figure there. There was a young woman leaning on the table wearing a loosely draped garment that allowed her back to be fully exposed. Tattooed on her back was a map. The map seemed accurate, familiar, but it was also fantastic. There were monsters and magical beasts, realms that were hidden or unknown all depicted in the midst of the familiar continents and labels.

When I woke, I wished I had the skill to draw what I had dreamt, it was fascinating and beautiful, but there was also an ominous feeling that lingered from that dark, lantern lit space. This dream is one that taps on my shoulder from time to time. I am still intrigued by those spaces on the map that are not on any map. Maps are a recurring theme for me, not only treasure maps or GPS locations, but also maps like you'd see at a park or camp, those placards sitting at the beginning or split in a path. Maps are intriguing on so many levels. These maps in my dreams always point to literal locations but there is a fantasy or more figurative location just beyond the page, sign, or paper.

This, again, is not so far outside of the experience of maps in waking life. Even with the advancements in satellite technology and scientific scans, there are places that are still unknown to us as a human species. Furthermore, there are things that one will encounter in any location that can never be shown navigationally, there will always be elements that come up "out of the blue." This term seems fitting as it originally referred to the appearance of thunder or lightning out of a clear blue sky, an unexpected weather event (Tréguer, 2017). So many people in the world today conflate strange weather occurrences with climate, climate change can certainly increase or intensify weather, but local weather (like a blizzard during a record setting year of global heat) cannot accurately "map" the climate emergency and can often serve to confuse, conflate, or conceal the data.

This can be especially important from a policy perspective as those who do not live in an area dealing with the immediate or obvious effects of climate chaos may not be as motivated to address the greater issue. Their constituents may not be as motivated to call for the needed changes and progressive actions to affect a global initiative. This, again, is what so much of the dissent at COP28 was railing against. "Because the power to control uncertainty is very unequally distributed, the greatest burden of uncertainties tends to fall on the weakest, with the fewest resources to withstand it" (Marris, 1996, p. 1). This was certainly what we are seeing today in terms of so many uncertainties in our society, especially in terms of the environment. At COP28, day one, the loss and damage fund was agreed to. This was an ambitious and, if they follow through, historic step to address this inequality of uncertainty.

Of course, with the climate emergency, there are uncertainty monsters lurking around every corner. Even high-income countries need to work to improve equity within their policy, environmental justice should be taken into account at all turns. There are people and communities who are being impacted disproportionately by pollution, a lack of funds to mitigate or adapt to a changing climate, and inadequate access to healthcare and other resources that could help address some of the multiple effects that climate change will continue to bring. The COVID-19 pandemic is one example of this, a changing climate brings humans into contact with wildlife as habitats become less and less suited. As you can see, this is an extremely complex issue from a scientific perspective, when you throw in political, cultural, economic, health, and psychological issues, it becomes even more so. The other reality of this is that none of these can be addressed alone. Policy especially, can affect various aspects of this for individuals and society at large.

Just like the explorers of yore, we find ourselves upon *terra incognita* in multiple ways. Maps of antiquity show many aspects in common with that map I saw tattooed in my dream. Certainly, there were no actual dragons or kraken, but there were reefs and ice floes that may have been a threat beyond comprehension at that point in time. These maps were a good starting point, they allowed others to come after to create better versions and find more efficient methods. This is the same issue many in the sciences experience and have a challenging time explaining. There is an element of uncertainty that must be confronted, like those mysterious and terrible places on the map, the "uncertainty monster" (Van der Sluijs, 2005) has to be confronted in public discourse.

In their paper "Climate Science and the Uncertainty Monster," meteorologist and climatologists Peter Webster and Judith Curry (2011) start out by addressing a similar feeling: "While extending the knowledge frontier often reduces uncertainty, it leads inevitably to a greater uncertainty as unanticipated complexities are discovered" (p. 1667). There is a certain sense of an evolving map here, stretching frontiers and discovery. The more science discovers, the more things have a possibility of change. The more corners of the world humanity discovered, the more the maps evolved, with new data came new theories and knowledge. What is important is to remain humble in the face of this uncertainty and to be as upfront as possible about what remains unsure.

In working with dreams, I feel my capacity to hold uncertainty has grown. I can recognize certain patterns and know that there are common interpretations of images, but I also hold this lightly, knowing it is subject to change. As I change, many of my dream images have remained my companions.

I look back at them now, from where I am in my life at this moment, and it's as if I am seeing them from an entirely new perspective. In reading Jung's *Red Book* and *Black Books*, I feel the same. Though they were written over a century ago, the images remain incredible alive and relevant in this era. Art seems to have a way of breaking through uncertainty by giving into it fully.

A piece of art can be reinterpreted in myriad ways, just like a dream image. Whoever encounters it will see it differently, they will imagine a meaning that may or may not have been intended by the artist. Though the painting, story, poem, or sculpture will always be the same, each person will read the same words, each encounter the same image, everything outside of that is up to interpretation and imagination. Their uncertainty can be a lesson to us even when confronting things that feel like they need to be more certain.

Unfortunately, data cannot be held in the same way. Science, though there is room for interpretation, to a point, the main uncertainty lies around the data and how to communicate it rather than within it. When a scientist pulls a core of ice from an Antarctic glacier, that ice, and the compounds found within it will always be the same. However, as technology improves, scientists may be able to interpret it via these new lenses. Similarly, taking that climatological data from the past and placing it in comparison with modern models will show us where we are in relation to time. What may have looked like a mostly straight line on a graph, when added to the knowledge we have today, becomes a growing curve. Nothing else about it has changed, only our view and understanding of it in these new contexts. Of course, even this analysis as someone outside of the hard sciences, is subject to uncertainty and loss. My analysis of these ideas are made from my viewpoint, through the lenses of Jungian and archetypal psychology. From that perspective, these seem to me strange reflections of one another that both hold their own types of ambiguity and loss.

In their paper, Curry and Webster conclude that "integrity is to the uncertainty monster as garlic is to a vampire" (2011, p. 1679). They also cite recommendations from a talk given by statistician Sir David Spiegelhalter (2010) for dealing with uncertainty by using "clear language to honestly communicate deeper uncertainties with due humility and without fear" and noting that "for public confidence, trust is more important than certainty." Curry and Webster also note that especially dealing with climate change, due to its elevated level of politicization, integrity is key (p. 1679). Note that their paper was written over a decade ago, in that time, the climate crisis has only become more evident and important, while it has become further polarized and politicized. "While the uncertainty monster will undoubtedly evolve and even grow, it can be tamed through understanding and acknowledgement, and we can learn to live with it by adapting our policies to explicitly include uncertainty" (Curry & Webster, 2011, p. 1679). The uncertainty monster must be brought into conscious awareness, like a figure from a nightmare it has to be confronted and brought into the light, otherwise its frightening power chases us all, unchecked, and in a panic.

Wayfinding

To authentically and humbly discuss the possibilities, fears, and losses that accompany uncertainty can be a balm to the monster. When we encounter uncertainty, especially in an area that seems like it should be more reliable, it can provoke extreme anxiety. "Anxieties provoke blame, intolerance, and defensive exclusion … and create a volatile politics full of new uncertainties" (Marris, 1996, p. 3). This is a sort of political feedback loop, as uncertainty rises, political discord increases, this further amplifies the unreliability of the world surrounding us, and the loop continues over and over intensifying with each return. Our defenses against this are serving to protect that conservative viewpoint mentioned earlier.

There is something especially virulent in this view, that the uncertainty beast has brought to light in the United States during this COVID-19 pandemic. It is a pattern we can see in climate issues and so many others as well. In the United States, the idea of "freedom" is perpetuated very strongly. "With freedom and justice for all" is the last line to the pledge of allegiance many Americans learned in school and continue to recite today at public or political gatherings. "There is an inherently inegalitarian logic to the control of uncertainty which constantly impels us towards a competitive struggle for autonomy, as each tried to protect [their] freedom of action while constraining others" (Marris, 1996, p. 5). Sadly, increasingly these days people seem to believe that their freedoms are only available to them by taking the same away from others.

In the case of coronavirus, and other, burgeoning infectious diseases, masking and other mitigation strategies were seen by many as an infringement on their rights and freedoms, rather than a reciprocal act of care for those most at risk to harm. We see this in other ways too, political messaging plays this out over and over, if taxes are raised it is not shown as needed collective action toward a more functional and secure society, but rather a diminishment of personal spending power or autonomy. When there are moves to cut fossil fuel emissions, it is rarely shown as an opportunity to reduce harm to the global community but rather that individuals will be denied their choice to drive what they want or cook on a gas burning stove. On the deeper level, this all comes down to the uncertainty of these situations. No one wants to acknowledge that we are confronting a pandemic that killed millions, a virus that continues to maim and harm disproportionately, or the possibility that they can be one of those effected. The same is true regarding climate.

One of the main defensive reactions here can be to seek scapegoats, to "turn inward" and "reinforce inequalities" (Marris, 1996, pp. 4–5). When we are faced with uncertainty or ambiguity, it can seem so much easier to put our issues on some "other": another group of people, part of the world, or individual. In this way countries and political entities can say that they are doing what they can, but when an agreement isn't reached or goals go untouched, they place the blame elsewhere. We can see this in the argument that there are lower income countries that still rely on burning coal as they develop their economies and infrastructure, while higher income countries continue to drill offshore and dig liquid natural gas (LNG) pipelines to export. Neither action is helpful to the climate crisis, we need to cut all coal and fossil fuel use. But to cast blame on others, while ignoring your own shortcomings is extremely harmful. In analytical psychology this seems very closely tied to the idea of projection. We do not want to see our own shortcomings, however, when we encounter someone who is expressing what we work so hard to repress or who is demonstrating the aspect we need, it can be endlessly triggering. "We try to withdraw to familiar certainties or fall into despair" (Marris, 1996, p. 1). We would much rather just mark that person as mean or annoying, disregard what they may have to offer us, or remove ourselves to wallow in self-pity. In both areas we prefer a return to business as usual, this is much more certain and requires far less work.

In this inward and outward comparison, we need to see that there is room for improvement in all areas and those with the most resources should work to redistribute funds to those who need it, rather than scapegoating them for a problem that they have very little to do with but bear the brunt of the ill effects. With the ongoing threat of COVID, this could be expressed through masking, especially in healthcare settings, where those most at risk need the most protection, Through funds for continued testing, vaccinations, treatment, and research into the ongoing effects of long-COVID. Further, better infrastructure funded on the community or national level to improve air quality in public spaces could keep us all safer from not only known, but also the possibility of emerging, novel, and unknown future illness.

This view is also one that the loss and damage fund at COP28 is pointing us to and that an increased emphasis on adaptation could move us toward in many sectors. A forward look, embracing uncertainty rather than denying it, has the possibility of creating "a more hopeful politics of collaboration and reciprocity" (Marris, 1996, p. 3). We need to look to all the paths ahead, take everyone who may be affected into consideration, and find a way forward that leaves no one behind. The map to the future may be littered with "uncertainty monsters," but we have a way forward that could lead to a brand-new landscape. This new realm is one of reciprocity, inclusion, authenticity, humility, and integrity.

For science, this seems to mean we need to take into account all the different models and understand fully that none of them will be "true." They will all contain reliable data that can point a way, but as we adapt to and hopefully mitigate the worst effects, these models will change too, the path will always evolve as we move nearer or farther to one uncertain future than another. For policy, all these possible futures must be taken into account. The way forward has to be based on the best data, honoring the uncertainty. There is an ambiguity there, but what can we lose by planning for the worst? By moving forward anticipating the very real possibility that our "North Star" of 1.5°C has passed us by, at worst, we make life better for whatever time we have for billions of people with infrastructure, social services, and economic assistance that is already badly needed. Note that, as of January 2024, we have confirmation of the first year averaging close to or at 1.5 according to the Copernicus Climate Change Service. We can write a new story, one that is fast, fair, funded, and phases out those things which no longer serve, and brings those who are marginalized to the front of all needed dialogue and negotiations.

In my personal story and dreams I hope to embody this. I have placed all these aspirations in my backpack on this trail. As I move my way through these overlapping maps of *Jung, Politics and Culture*, the best I can do is know that I will fall short, but I will put forward these super-imposed ideas with as much authenticity as I can. One of the most striking gifts I got from my dreams as my mother was hospitalized was the one that dreams and art can give us all, the ability to see from multiple perspectives. In many of these dreams I was in many places at once, seeing myself interacting while watching others around us. Even the most minor character in a dream is a part of my psyche, an aspect of myself. This same character is also the embodiment of an other that I may or may not know in waking life. They hold characteristics of others out in the world today, experiencing things I may never come into contact with outside of the dreamscape.

I do not dismiss these pieces of myself or society, rather, I lean into them. I wonder who they are and what things are like from where they stand. I wander into that space, put on their shoes, view the world from their perspective. This is the gift of empathy that dreams allow each of us. In Figure 1, my north star is seen from a dream within the aperture of a camera lens. It reminds me that this is one perspective, that though my perspective is mine alone, it is in its way, representative of many others, each of us connected by our uniqueness. Navigating toward this North Star, one of care and understanding, I find my way to a place where I can set my own comforts and freedoms aside to imagine how I can best be in service to those who I may never meet, but who I can imagine with compassion, empathy, and love. Finally, I wait. I wait for a day when others see things this way too. In this waiting, I find the way forward is not passive, but incredibly active. Just like the North Star that stands still, everything else continues to move around it, even in times of waiting there is movement if we can expand our perspective.

We can only see a glacier move by waiting or tracking its retreat from year to year or decade to decade. Coral only spawns once a year under the most ideal conditions, the other 11 months, they wait and grow. For the pyrophyte, as type of seed, it waits to burn before it can break free from its shell and grow. For each of us, wherever we are, this waiting can be more or less active. For those on the front lines, the waiting can be frustrating and too long in coming,

Figure 1 Drawing, *Guiding Aperture*, colored pencil on paper, by the author.

this waiting must find moments of radical rest to prevent burnout. Waiting holds despair and hope, loss and gain, forward and backward, like a rising tide. In tackling these complex, chaotic, ambiguous, and uncertain moments, to wait is to hold space. To hold space for all the possibilities, the worst and the best, and to find a way to move forward. To hold space to give all the voices time to speak, to wait into the unknown, hear the stories that need to be told and imagine new tales to meet the world anew.

Resources

Boss, P. (1999). *Ambiguous loss: Learning to live with unresolved grief.* Harvard University Press.

Boss, P. (2006). *Loss, trauma, and resilience: Therapeutic work with ambiguous loss.* W.W. Norton and Company.

Copernicus Climate Change. (2024, January 9). *Copernicus: 2023 is the hottest year on record, with global temperatures close to the 1.5 C limit* [Press release]. https://climate.copernicus.eu/copernicus-2023-hottest-year-record

Curry, J., & Webster, P. (2011). Climate science and the uncertainty monster. In *Bulletin for the American Meteorological Society, 92*(12) (pp. 1667–1682). https://www.researchgate.net/publication/258488239_Climate_Science_and_the_Uncertainty_Monster

Harper, D (2024). Doom. In *Online Etymology Dictionary.* https://www.etymonline.com/word/doom

Jung, C. G. (2020). *The black books: 1913–1932 notebooks of transformation, Vol. 4.* (In S. Shamdasani, Ed.). (M. Liebscer, J. Peck, & S. Shamdasani, Trans.). W.W. Norton and Company.

Marris, P. (1996). *Politics of uncertainty: Attachment in private and public life.* Routledge.

Marris, P. (2014). *Loss and change* (Psychology Revivals: Revised Edition). Taylor and Francis. (Original work published 1974.)

Mecklin, J. (Ed.). (2024, January 23). *2024 doomsday clock announcement.* Bulletin of the Atomic Scientists. https://thebulletin.org/doomsday-clock/current-time/

Mehta, L., & Srivastava, S. (2020). Uncertainty in modelling climate change: The possibilities of co-production through knowledge pluralism. In I. Scoones & A. Stirling (Eds.), *The politics of uncertainty: Challenges of transformation (Pathways to sustainability)* (p. 99). Taylor and Francis.

Merriam-Webster, Incorporated. (2023). On 'doomsurfing' and 'doomscrolling': Can you think of a better way to spend your time? [Words we're watching]. *Merriam-Webster.com.* https://www.merriam-webster.com/wordplay/doomsurfing-doomscrolling-words-were-watching

Spiegelhalter, D. (2010). *Quantifying uncertainty* [audio file]. https://web.archive.org/web/20110815024547/https://downloads.royalsociety.org/audio/DM/DM2010_03/Speigelhalter.mp3

Tréguer, P. (2017, July 14). The authentic origin of 'out of the blue.' In *Word Histories.* https://wordhistories.net/2017/07/14/out-of-the-blue-origin/

van der Sluijs, J. P. (2005). Uncertainty as a monster in the science–policy interface: Four coping strategies. In *Water Science & Technology, 52* (pp. 87–92). DOI:10.2166/wst.2005.0155

2 Entangled in Viscous Tides

The concept of "global warming," though a scientifically accurate description of our changing climate, is one that has been debated and often misconstrued. I know I have seen the threads going around social media in years past, "How can there be global warming when its freezing cold where I live?" even in recent years, with the extreme polar vortices so many experienced, the same old narrative emerged trying to discredit the idea of a warming planet, acknowledging the unruly changes to the weather in a way that completely separates it from the larger picture. This is part of the uncertainty monster rising from the deep.

In the realm of uncertainty, this can make its own strange "sense." Global warming is a massively large systems-based theory of the climate. There are so many parts and pieces connected in myriad ways, it's hard to explain to the average citizen of the world why the changes in ocean temperatures can affect the movement of the atmosphere high above which can lead to seemingly random changes and extremities in the weather here, but not there. I hope you have already gotten a sense of that up to this point. There are so many threads that weave together in this climate crisis. In his 2013 book *Hyperobjects: Philosophy and Ecology after the End of the World*, Timothy Morton stated that global warming is a "hyperobject." By this he means that it is something "massively distributed in time and space relative to humans" (p. 1).

In Morton's (2013) exploration, hyperobjects are "viscous," in that they stick to everything. The more one tries to escape, the more glued to the object one becomes; they are so large they dispute any concept of fixedness or concreteness; they are "nonlocal" meaning they are distributed throughout time and space such that they are infinitely complex and interconnect a multiplicity of factors; they are "phased" in such a way they occupy a space beyond regular perception; and they are "interobjective," a quality Morton describes by explaining that they are relational, one can only recognize a hyperobject by the footprint it leaves, by the other factors it holds, influences, and connects to (pp. 26–95). Often, one can only begin to recognize a hyperobject by the charts and graphs of data collected over a great period of time. We can begin to see from the previous chapter, why the climate crisis would fit into this

DOI: 10.4324/9781032644820-3

category, the need to model and use historical data to track the changes is an integral piece in this realm, no matter the uncertainty they may present.

In reading about hyperobjects, I heard the flowing of depth psychological streams. The hyperobject felt very archetypal for me. There was a distinct parallel to how archetypal energies help us to recognize and relate to the archetypes per se. In myth, fairy tales, and many artistic, cultural products, we encounter the archetypal. These can be figures or concepts that have a core emotion or energy that remains consistent across cultures and across time. We can know and interact with many faces of the archetype in dreams and in the other areas mentioned above. However, there is no way to see the "true" face of them, their guise changes dependent on who encounters them and when. We can encounter archetypal images locally, but acausally. They are outside our time and space and beyond our typical realm of perception, and if ignored, only cry out louder and stronger to be heard, sticking to our conscious memory in drips and drabs that we collect from dreams, synchronicities, and the like. In his further explanation of hyperobjects, Morton posits that they become visible during this age of ecological crisis to alert us to the dilemma we are facing.

I feel the same about this issue, whether it is a hyperobject, an archetype, or something both/and and in between, the face of this issue, the image that "stuck" with me through the years is Ice. I capitalize it here to emphasize the archetypal and relational experience I had with this image. Ice became my constant companion and for me, the object that represented climate change most clearly. This is not only because of the obvious depletion of the cryosphere (the areas of our planet where ice has been a constant presence) on a warming planet. Ice is intimately connected to so many systems and tipping points, it has often been called the "canary in the coalmine" of the climate emergency. Even on top of all these scientific explanations, Ice embodies so much of what we need to embrace when facing the uncertainties of this warming world.

No doubt you will find ice and Ice scattered throughout these pages, though I will stop the capitalization, know that ice is, in my view, a symbol in the Jungian sense, it points to the archetypal. It is what it is, but it is also something much more, something that holds mystery and wonder, an object or subject that points to something much deeper and wider than we may see at first glance. This is the truth of ice. Ice is much more than what we see on the surface. The ice of glaciers can hold the history of our planet, it is a great library of the past. Scientists core ice in various parts of the world to gather atmospheric and other data to create models and track changes over centuries. Ice on a dark road may be merely frozen water, but it can also be a deadly and uncertain threat. Snow is microscopic ice crystals that hold a sense of wonder and play, memories of snow days and holidays for some. When compacted together these tiny ice crystals can present a threat and, nevertheless, in all these guises and more, they were my guide and traveling companion through the heavy work that is researching climate catastrophe.

Figure 2 Drawing, *Iceberg in Shades of Blue and Silver*, colored pens, marker, and ink on paper, by the author.

When I was involved in my graduate studies at Pacifica Graduate Institute, we had a course on Imaginal Knowing and Jung's Red Book. One of the guest lecturers was author and depth psychologist, Robert Romanyshyn. In class that afternoon, he showed us a short film he created called *Antarctica*, it was a composite of video and images from a trip to the titular continent. He included voiceovers throughout that were poetic and moving. It was, to me, a dream on film. I was completely captivated by the images. I felt a deep sorrow within, one that was my own, but at the same time far beyond myself. This was a grief that took me right into the depths of ice.

As we finished up the film, Romanyshyn asked us to take some time on our own to reflect and connect with what we just watched. We were told to find a place in the room where we could be on our own and to take a pose that would embody whatever we were feeling. As I found my quiet corner, I knelt. I felt my hands move into a position of prayer, my head bowed, and I began to weep. This rising tide of tears was overwhelming and shocking. I could not stop crying. These tears were spilling out from my heart, it was as if those images of the ice had melted and cracked something open within me. I knew there was something more, I felt a call and a purpose in those tears.

As the year went on, I studied everything I could about the melting ice and climate change. I had always been environmentally minded; I was that kid in middle school who was in "Earth Club" making sure we were recycling and saving the whales. From a very young age, even when the climate discourse was somewhat nascent, at least to the general public, I felt a pull to help wherever I could. Back then it was mostly "reduce, reuse, recycle" (with the green triangle of arrows) and endangered species (generally a Panda or a whale) that held the narrative, but it always felt like there was more to it than these surface signs of warning.

The months I spent with ice prepared me in a strange way for what was to come. In Chapter 1, the experience of ambiguous loss with my mother, her weeks in a coma and subsequent long recovery, had the container of ice to hold them. In going through that experience of loss and uncertainty, I realized that I had been prepared for the journey by my icy explorations. I was sitting at the hospital bed of ice, waiting for what may come. This waiting with ice gave me a vessel to hold the uncertainty of those long weeks by my mother's bedside. At the same time, as I traveled through the prolonged process of recovery and eventual acceptance of our new normal, I found that I learned more about how one might approach the uncertain future we all face as the climactic emergency surges forward.

This was an extraordinarily complex and tangled experience, there are still many pieces of my life that I don't think will ever be extricated from the grief and trauma of that time. I also know from that difficult period that a time of ambiguity and uncertainty can seem unbearable, and a sure path forward is much more attractive than a foggy road ahead. In my processes of grief both personal and planetary, the five stages laid out by Elisabeth Kubler-Ross (2011) seemed to come all at once. As soon as I could see a strand of "acceptance" it would become knotted with "denial, anger, bargaining, depression" (p. 287), and the like.

Though it seems promising to have five or seven stages of grief to work through systematically, that is arguably never the way grief works. Inevitably we get lost and tangled along the way. Each path forward loops back upon itself and one day we find ourselves back on the same road, but hopefully a little farther along than when we were forced to detour. The same is true for the strange journey toward whatever lies ahead for us on this changing planet. The challenges we face are multifaceted and interwoven.

In the recent publication *Earth for All: A Survival Guide for Humanity*, (Dixson-Decleve et al, 2022), the authors explain the many paths forward we might take. They imagine the outcome of ambitious policy and the devastation of "business as usual." In a strange parallel to the ideas of grief above, this book lays out five areas where policy can be addressed to make the most meaningful change in the face of climate uncertainty. These are policies that address "poverty, inequality, gender equity, food, and energy" (p. 171).

Just as with my experience of grief in the face of ambiguous loss, all five stages need to occur at the same time. There needs to be a both/and approach to these ideas, an everything, everywhere view. Climate action, especially on the policy level, has to risk becoming entangled in order to find a way through. Most of the ideas in *Earth for All* (E4A) (Dixson-Decleve et al, 2022) are based on economic assessments and the recommendations rely on a massive overhaul of our economic system, the general areas of reform are sufficient to give the breadth of the change that is needed: #1 poverty, #2 inequality, #3 gender equity, #4 food, and #5 energy. If we agree with Morton that global warming is a hyperobject, an equally systemic and multiple solution must be sought.

As was mentioned in the introduction, this series, Jung, Politics and Culture, points to all these levels of scholarship, it is a transdisciplinary approach, interweaving and untangling threads to find a point of commons. In that spirit, I'd like to bring in a folktale from Greenland: Sassuma Arnaa (Mother of the Sea). She is also known as Sedna, Mother of the Deep, Arnakuagsak or Arnaqquassaaq, among other names (Kristjánsdóttir, 2020). As is the way with folktales, there are pieces that are uniform no matter the telling, but the telling I heard may differ from the telling of other elders.

I pull my knowledge of this tale from a short film put forward by Waterbear, a streaming platform with a mission to save the planet through impactful film. They have a series of short films called *Living Stories* and this one is *Mother of the Sea (Sassuma Arnaa)* (Brown & Ingemann, 2021). Throughout the film the tale is told in Kalaallisut by a number of Indigenous Greenlandic Inuit elders and children from Uummannaq. Amid wide landscape shots, it is animated in a beautifully strange torn paper, mixed media, stop motion style. In the background traditional throat singing, wind instruments, sounds of ice cracking, ocean waves, and haunting wind blows. The story goes something like this:

> *There was a young woman who married a magical man, he was half man, half bird and they lived far away in the mountains. One day she begins missing her family, somehow, her father hears about this and decides to bring her family to rescue her. They are able to get her into their boat and head home. Unfortunately, her husband realizes what is happening and he summons a storm to capsize their boat. In an effort to save the family, the father throws the young woman overboard to appease the bird-man, stop*

the storm, and save his family. His daughter does not want to return to her husband, so she grips the side of the boat, refusing to let go. So, her father chops her fingers off with an axe.

She falls into the ocean, sinks to the bottom, and each of her severed fingers turns into an animal. "Whale, polar bear, seal, fish, shark ... All the animals of the sea come from her severed fingers" (Brown, N. & Ingemann, U., 2021). *Since she has no fingers to comb her long hair, it becomes tangled in the ocean currents and begins to trap all the animals and fish, so no one above the water can have a good hunt or catch. Whenever the catch is scarce, the shamans must travel into the depths to comb her hair, soothe her, and release the animals.*

In the film a few of the storytellers note that in our world today, we must improve our relationship with the mother of the sea and with our planet. The more she is agitated by plastics, pollution, and more, the more tangled her hair becomes and the scarcity of the hunt and fishing increases. Though combing her hair is the realm of the shamans, how we each behave and treat the sea can affect how Sedna in turn treats us.

The beauty of folktales is that they tell a truth that is separate from facts, but a factual interpretation is not always so far away either, it is both/and. I often like to work with myths and folktales as if they are a dream I woke up with. This is an archetypal view, one where Jungian symbols come to life and make us wonder. As is the way with dreams, we can see them in many lights. Dreams have not only a personal level, but collective and archetypal levels. They pull from our past and can point to the future.

This tale is rife with grief. Sedna, in this one, short story, goes through all five stages of grief. She refuses to submit to her husband and accept her isolated fate (denial). She clings to the side of the boat, crying to be saved (bargaining). She sinks to the bottom of the ocean (depression). She becomes so frustrated; she is entangled in everything around her (anger). Eventually, she is soothed and lives into this role of mother of the sea, her separated fingers becoming nourishment for all those above (acceptance). However, this tale is passed from generation to generation, so the cycle never ends. At every moment, she is in a single stage and entangled in them all simultaneously. This is the nature of grief.

This tale, as with all good fairy tales and folktales, has many levels. Though Sedna is "Mother of the Sea" she is also a representation of Mother Earth in many ways. Even in the film, the narration makes this larger move. With systems theory and the worldwide interconnection of ecosystems, warming, ocean currents, and more, this is not too far off the mark. To look at Sedna's story as a tale for Earth today we see each stage of her life as one we are confronting daily and ones that echo *Earth for All*'s (Dixson-Decleve et al, 2022) policy recommendations and the chants at COP28 for a fast, fair, feminist, phase out.

At the start of the story, we see Sedna caught in a bargain that no longer works for her, she is in debt to the bird-man. In some of the tellings of this tale

I came across, she was offered to her bridegroom against her will. Her father is most often the one who exchanged her for something else of value, food, resources, some material exchange. She is devalued and cast out, left repaying someone else's debt. This, as we hear at the most recent COP, is the way many countries in the global South, Indigenous populations, youth, and the poor worldwide feel—exchanged for the prosperity of others and then left behind.

Sedna is entangled and also entangles. She is an indigenous voice, a woman, cast out of society, uncared for, disabled, and forgotten. She falls into all the marginalized areas of concern in our world today. In their report, E4A note that when they mention gender equity, and in the chants of a "feminist" plan forward at COP, the inference is that these need to be intersectional (Crenshaw, 1989) and apply to "all marginalized groups…indigenous groups and refugees" as well as anyone "discriminated against for reasons of race, sexual orientation, religion, income, and so on" (p. 94). Sedna in our world today is all of these. She is a symbol of this needed intersectionality.

In Kimberlé Crenshaw's (1989) definition, intersectionality is an experience that is a "complex phenomenon" that "is greater than the sum of racism and sexism" (p. 140). It is another area where a both/and approach is needed. Crenshaw initially coined this term to address the experience of Black women, too often overlooked or underrepresented in spaces where laws, policies, or movements were only focused on the experience of those who fell into a single category. Her argument was, as someone who transcends, overlaps, is entangled in more than one minority experience, her unique identification was underrepresented. The definition is wide enough to apply to anyone and everyone who falls into this space of overlap, those who are BIPOC (Black, Indigenous, Persons of Color), LGBTQIA+ (Lesbian, Gay, Bisexual, Transgender, Queer/questioning, Intersex, Asexual, and more), those who are otherly-abled, and further marginalized groups in various combinations.

We have become increasingly entangled in all the ways our modern world has treated Sedna in her multiple forms today. The gifts of Earth are dwindling because of this entanglement, our dismissal of her needs, and what this represents in the environmental uncertainty that we face as a world community. What this tale illustrates so beautifully is the interconnected nature of these forgotten influences, the "other" deep in the unconscious who needs to be cared for and connected to. This is important from a depth psychological perspective, where we hope to bring the contents of the unconscious into dialogue for a better understanding of ourselves and, in my experience, the world around us. It is equally important in issues like global warming, where there is not a single policy or path forward that will work for everyone involved. It is tangled up and uncertain.

As E4A notes, there is a debt to be paid and a lot of debt to be forgiven, we need a just transition. A few examples of the policies suggested to address these areas are debt cancelation for low-income countries, increasing taxes on the 10% richest, strengthening workers' rights, providing access to education for women and girls, and achieving gender equity in jobs and leadership

(p. 171). As we can see, they are not small shifts, these would be massively important policy changes on a scale that could benefit the whole world, they are "extraordinary turnarounds" (p. 21). In E4A's description of these, and to illustrate the complexity, they show a five-pointed star. Each of these turnarounds is one point, at the top is empowerment, then, clockwise moves to inequality, energy, food, and poverty. Each section is connected to the others with an entanglement of arrows, creating a sort of interwoven tapestry of connection between the five points (p. 21).

Interestingly at COP28, as mentioned in the introduction, we can see a faint outline of the acknowledgement of the moves needed to honor an intersectional and just path forward, slowly beginning to take shape. There were historical discussions of loss and damage, high-income countries paying toward lower-income countries. Though these do not point to current debt relief, they do suggest the debt owed to those most harshly and immediately affected. Perhaps these five points could represent a new "north star" (especially now that we know 1.5°C is a reality and has been for the past year) for not only tackling climate change generally, but for making the way forward just and equitable, honoring all five points of the E4A star and all the entangled, complexity this holds. A north star to remind us that the way forward must contain multitudes, how the differences that want to divide us can offer areas of compassion and empathy, and only by honoring the intersection of all cultures and individuals, can we begin to untangle our future from the neglects of our past.

Resources

Brown, N., & Ingemann, U. (Directors). (2021). *Living stories: Mother of the sea (Sassuma Arnaa)* [Short Film]. Waterbear.

Crenshaw, K. (1989). Demarginalizing the intersection of race and sex: A Black feminist critique of antidiscrimination doctrine, feminist theory and antiracist politics. In *The University of Chicago legal forum 1989:139* (pp. 139–167). https://philpapers.org/archive/CREDTI.pdf

Dixson-Decleve, S., Gaffney, O., Ghosh, J., Randers, J., Rockstrom, J., & Stoknes, P.E. (2022). *Earth for all: A survival guide for humanity*. New Society Publishers.

Kristjánsdóttir, A. O. (2020, August 13). "Mother of the Sea" in Greenlandic myths and legends [blog post] on *Greenland adventures*. https://www.greenland.is/blog/greenlandic-myths-and-legends/

Kubler-Ross, E. (2011). *On death and dying: What the dying have to teach doctors, nurses, clergy and their own families*. Scribner.

Morton, T. (2013). *Hyperobjects: Philosophy and ecology after the end of the world*. University of Minnesota Press.

3 Shadows of Green Shroud Fires of Change

Shadows of Green

In my imagination, the wandering, entangling, fog of the climate question is held in shades of green. From the blue-green oceans to forest hues, whenever I hear someone casually mention something climate related, green is not far behind. Politically, there is the divisive "Green New Deal," Green Party, or a Green Movement. There is also the issue of greenwashing, where companies appear more invested in initiatives to support climate mitigation than they actually are. They can also greenwash more literally by choosing packaging with green labels or nature images to show they are eco-conscious, when very few ingredients or manufacturing standards align with that goal.

Now we find that the green arrows on the recycling bins are a greenwashing all their own, very few plastics can be recycled and even those that may be reused in some ways are instead being shipped overseas, to become someone else's trash. This fraud was uncovered and reported by the Center for Climate Integrity in February of 2024 (Allen et al., 2024). The authors of this study report that the petrochemical companies were well aware that their products could not be recycled but continued "carrying out a well-coordinated campaign to deceive consumers, policymakers, and regulators" for more than 50 years (p. 4). This is that strange green fog of uncertainty, but one that leans into distrust and deception, the green of monetary enrichment clinging to every breath.

I find this fog within the smoke of wildfires as well. The green symbolism of the trees carried forward into the grey poisonous smoke. Certainly, there have been wildfires prior to our industrial age, but the levels of planetary heating, drought, deforestation, and the like, fueled by mass industrialization and corporate greed contribute again to the greening of the fog. I find this fog in the sickening pollution from manufacturing plants on the edge of front-line communities. Most of which are home to people of color, Indigenous populations, and/or those who are poor or economically below the poverty line. I find this fog in the many unseen pollutants in our world today, from pesticides, to pandemics, to plastics. This is a putrid green of pollution which ranges from air, to water, to light, to sound, and more.

DOI: 10.4324/9781032644820-4

We know, as of recent scientific reports, that plastics can be anything from what you can see littering highways and beaches, to much smaller microplastics, and virtually invisible nanoplastics, a complex mix, each with a unique "environmental fate and behavior" (ter Halle and Ghiglione, 2021). Each of these holds uncertainty and green. A greening that is living in every cell of our bodies. A greening that can offer us moments of self-reflection amidst the fog. A green that is so multiple and complex that we if we can learn to move within, separating its gifts from its curses, we may begin to find a better way forward. A number of years ago, I had the following dream, interestingly, this dream contained another tattoo, there is something of our current crisis that gets under my skin apparently:

> *I just got a tattoo of the word "green," but it is written in a strange font or language that is mostly recognizable, but there is a lot of flourish and extra symbols within each letter. It reminds me of those Coexist bumper stickers, but none of the symbols are religious, at least not ones I recognize. It is on my right forearm near the bend of my elbow where one would have blood taken. I am showing it to someone when I realize there is a large piece of concrete nearby that has broken off of the building. The break reveals graffiti on the stone underneath. It is from many years ago, long before I was born, it is the same symbol that I just had tattooed.*

When I woke from this dream, I typed it up in my phone, as I try to do when my mornings allow, and I went about my day. But this idea of green would not leave me. I was part of an online writing group at the time, *Seeding Soul Stories*, and I brought it with me that week as a writing prompt. However, the night of, Figure 3 is what I ended up with in my notebook. An image of the tattoo, but more legible than it was in the dream and an amorphous green blob, a green circle edged by blues, some facets or starbursts showing in darker greens, giving a slight echo to a round, precious gem. This Green was content to remain elusive, clinging to the image, but still mysterious and unformed. It would be years before I started to scratch the surface.

One of the most gifted dream workers I have ever had the fortune of getting to know, the late Jeremy Taylor (1998), had a term for these dream images, the ones just can't quite put into words or bring into conversation. He would say that these were "not yet speech-ripe" (p. 263), held still in the grasp of the unconscious. Thus was the case with Green for me. So, I went about my day, my week, my month, and now, several years where this green has come to mind, but never found an outlet, it was stubbornly under-ripe. Honestly, what did I expect from Green? In nature, bananas, tomatoes, and many other fruits and vegetables show they are not quite ready for picking or eating when they are still green, in much the same way, this image of green needed to develop into its fullness.

Figure 3 A sketch from my dream notebook of the "green" tattoo and the green blob. Drawing, *Green Dream Mandala,* colored pencil on paper, by the author.

From time to time, I would think about this green. I looked it up in the *Dictionary of Symbols* (Chevalier & Gheerbrant, 1996/1969) and found a five-plus page entry, quite voluminous. I would read a piece every now and then, each time something new would strike true, but it always felt like there was something deeper. There was an ambiguity of green that I just couldn't put a finger on. I would often reflect on that dictionary entry. There, they noted there is the "fresh green of the buds of Spring" and the "green of slime and putrefaction: there is a death-green and a life-green" (Chevalier & Gheerbrant, 1996/1969, p. 454). They connected it to many deities or holy beings across various cultures: Al Kadir, the Green Man, Osiris, Xochiquetzal, the Green Lion, Vishnu, and many others who are themselves green, symbolized by, or connected to the color green (Chevalier & Gheerbrant, 1996/1969, pp. 451–455).

For me, amplifying the idea of green brought with it any number of associations, some of them I already introduced above. The green of nature, green space, greening a church for holy days; greenwashing, the green of American money and greed; green triangles of recycling, Green Parties in politics, green for luck, green for envy, the grass is always greener on the other side; green as land on a map, green for go, on and on and on. Green is multifaceted, like an intricately cut emerald, containing as many shades as the green iris of a cat's eye. Green is all this and more.

It had been quite a while since I dove back into the waters of this dream. But one morning, I was looking out the kitchen window, at the beautiful patch of wild nature we have growing freely as our backyard in our overly manicured neighborhood. Not surprisingly, it is always full of a variety of birds, a small family of bunnies, a mama deer and her two fawns, and occasionally a visiting mouse, fox, or opossum. At that time, the plants were returning from their winter sleep. All the trees and bushes and weeds popping in vibrant greens, so many shades of green! I began to think, what is it about green? And suddenly, this old friend of a dream floated by. I'm still not sure if it is ripe enough, however, since it has opened itself to further conversation, it feels as if something is shifting in our relationship. Green, for me, seems speech-ripe finally.

Green branded me with its mark, so it has never been far, even when it has gone silent. If I roll up my dream sleeve and offer it lifeblood, perhaps we will be able to find fertile ground to grow together. So, I went to my digital dream journal to find the original entry. I figured the best place to start is the first account. Wouldn't you know, I woke with my green dream on April 1, 2017, green has an affinity for April Fool's day, it seems they are quite the trickster. I have to say that I was not surprised to encounter this quality of green, as soon as the realization of this date flitted through my mind, galloping boisterously alongside, was the Green Knight, or the knight of the Green Chapel from the King Arthur tales.

Green has a "middling quality" (Chevalier & Gheerbrant, 1996/1969), it mediates and can cross boundaries, many of its embodied energies are psychopomps, those who can go between the conscious and the unconscious, between mortals and the divine. It has a dreamlike quality, just like the Green Knight. Interestingly, in the first edition of *Sir Gawain and the Green Knight* (Kirtlan, 1912/1360) (offered to the worldwide audience on Google books thanks to the Harvard Library), the book is dedicated "To my lady of dreams, my wife." Indeed, no matter the version, almost every aspect of the story could be a dream, flitting between the unconscious and consciousness, it is quite middling.

In the introduction of this first edition, the translator, Kirtlan (1912), writes "With aching heart and bleeding feet" we pursue "the phantoms of [our] dreams, only to find when" we stretch "out to grasp them, that [we] are wildly clutching at nothing" (pp. 1–2, pronouns changed to reflect a more inclusive population). The translator continues to introduce the King Arthur tales in the same way I would speak of a dream or myth. He suggests that these tales have become the "possession of universal humanity. Yet King Arthur probably never existed. And it is just because humanity's heart feels that he ought to have existed … the saga has completely saturated the soul of the world" (1912, p. 3). The ambiguity, uncertainty, and loss in these few words are staggering.

In these lines we see that not only the Green Knight in this tale, but also Arthur and his knights are both dead and alive, immortal and immediate. Though the worldwide appeal of this particular legend is probably overstated, from an archetypal perspective the possibility of this type of tale, the energetic and emotional effects of this style of story, is universal. There is a heroic and chaotic play in many diverse cultural tales and mythologies that could provide a parallel to this tale. For me, the tale of Gawain and the Green Knight is one I grew up with, it holds and held me in mystery and wonder, perhaps you have a favorite that you could tap into here as well?

In this tale, at a grand feast, the Green Knight bursts into Arthurs court. In a beautiful version by Charlton Miner Lewis, 1903, this is all set forth in poetic rhyme, the type one could imagine a fairytale trickster reciting. He galloped in with a blast of winter "on the empty air, a great green giant on a great green mare" (Lewis, Canto 1, Para. 6, 1903). At once flighty but, in the next sentence, heavy enough to deliver "an earthquake's jolt" Lewis, Canto 1, Para. 6, 1903. He has a spirit of play, "greenly laughing" (Lewis, Canto 1, Para. 6, 1903), but they soon find this is deadly business too. In every line he embodies and oozes green. From his eyes, to his clothes, his axe, and soon we discover, even is blood!

He exclaims that he brings adventure to the court and asks that someone strike him with his own axe on the condition that they will meet again in a year and a day whence he will respond in kind. The youngest in the court steps up to accept, it is Gawain, Arthur's nephew. But, before Gawain takes up the challenge, the sacrifice, he asks the giant where he should find him to keep this promise. The giant tells him "We'll speak of that, please, when you've struck your blow" (Lewis, 1903). Until the bargain is struck and the fatal blow endured, the being remains a mystery. With Arthur's approval the bargain is struck, "across the Green Knight's features there was seen to pass a fleeting shade of deeper green, whether of disappointment or resentment, none knew; but straight a smile of bright contentment" (Lewis, 1903, Canto 1, ¶16). Thus, the giant knight kneels and offers his neck. With one stroke, Gawain beheads him.

Instead of falling to this fate, the knight picks up his head, and, though dismembered, speaks: "At the Green Chapel by the Murmuring Mere I will await you when the sun sinks low, and pay you back full measure, blow for blow!" (Lewis, 1903, Canto 1, ¶21). The mysterious visitor turns, his horses' hooves strike green sparks from the floor and thus, "with a whirring flash of emerald light" (Lewis, 1903, Canto 1, ¶21), the covenant is struck, literally and figuratively, Gawain is bound to his fate in a year and a day. The giant mounts his horse, and reminding Gawain of his oath to meet again in a year, returns into the dark woods from where he came. Though the court plays along in jest, the axe is hung as a trophy, and Gawain's uncertain fate is sealed.

Though the other knights seem to dismiss the promise the Green Knight made, as thought waking from a dream, "the lords and ladies rubbed their eyes … the great hall echoed once more with … laughing" (Lewis, 1903, Canto 1, ¶22). Guinevere, Arthur's wife, seems worried. One can only imagine, for Gawain, the uncertainty before him must be unbearable. In the text, at the beginning of Lewis' Canto 3, we see the time has come: "A year passed by, as years are wont to do, Winter and spring, summer and autumn too" (¶2). So Gawain must set out to meet his fate. It seems in the court the reality is setting in "weeping ladies thronged around … and bid him sad farewell" (Lewis, 1903, Canto 1, ¶22). The Green Knight was calling from within the green woods and Gawain rode off, through cold and storm, day and night, until he reached the "heart of a dense willow-wood" (Lewis, 1903, Canto 1, ¶3).

Year after year, my dream called to me from these woods, silent, without thought or word, this Green had also lost its head, yet the promise we made was written on my body and in stone centuries before. Now is the time to face the deep green woods, face the axe and the trickster who wields it. This tale and my dream speak to me so much about our current times. I have often wondered about "Green." In our modern world, green is related to money and capitalism, but also to the environmental movement, what a tension of opposites. In ecology, green is not only a sign of new growth, but can also represent decay. Green is at once birth and death, old and new, greed and altruism. Green tells us when to go. However, if we are moving too fast, spinning in circles, or rocking the boat, we get "green in the gills" and green tells us it's time to stop. Green is the trickster at every turn.

I have heard it said that the human eye can see more shades of green than any other color. As I step into the murky depths of this medieval forest, I hope that this is true. Indeed, green, at the middle (that middling quality again) of our visible spectrum, makes it the easiest for human eyes to perceive (Jimison, 2017). We evolved in circumstances that made differentiating shades of green a helpful and necessary quality. For the tale, differentiation and discernment of the right path forward is essential. This is what I hope Green can show me as well. Eventually, we learn that the Green Knight is "an arch-magician over all" (Lewis, 1903, Canto 4, ¶2), in many versions of this tale he is given these gifts of transformation and magic by Morgan le Fey, Arthur's stepsister and sourcerer. In his disguises he could be standing right next to Gawain or miles away, and indeed he is both present and absent throughout.

As is the way in many fairytales, Gawain is thrice tested. He finds himself taking comfort in a castle on his way to the final blow. The lord of the house leaves to hunt every day. Each time he says he will gift Gawain with whatever he catches, if Gawain will gift him anything he receives while he is out. This tricky game seems to have echoes of a certain Knight, but if Gawain is aware, he does not seem to hint at it. Day after day, Gawain is tested in a dreamlike fog, "the perilous wiles of magic art" (Lewis, 1903, ¶12). The knight and Gawain share their daily conquests, it is part of their compact. On the last day though, Gawain, on top of his usual gift of a kiss from the enchanting mistress of the house, he is also given a magical green belt, girdle, or sash, to protect him from the blow of the axe. Holding it, he knows her words to be true, he can sense a strangeness in this simple object (Lewis, 1903, ¶20). At their ritual exchange, Gawain gives the knight his kiss, but does not reveal his other boon. Knowing he is to face the axe in the morning, Gawain does not want to risk the loss of this protection. On the final day, he must venture forth to the green chapel. This is the green of "the depths and of Fate" (Chevalier & Gheerbrant, 1996/1969, p. 456).

This "chapel" does not appear to have been made by human hands, it is a small knoll covered in weeds, surrounded by trees. "The place was a wild hollow, circled round with barren hills … moss-grown, solitary" (Lewis, 1903, Canto 4, ¶4). It is beautifully wild and embedded in nature, almost overcome by growth and dug into the depths of the earth. There he upholds his end of the bargain; he bears his neck and awaits the fatal blow. The Green Knight raises the axe to strike him, and Gawain cowers out of fear upon the first pass. After some playful chiding, Gawain promises to "hold as still as death" (Lewis, 1903, Canto 4, ¶4). He is true to his word and seems to almost become embedded in the greens around him, the second blow is again in jest, but third the Green Knight let his axe fall "and lightly grazed Sir Gawayne's neck. He felt the hot blood flow, and saw red drops that sank deep in the snow" (Lewis, 1903, Canto 4, ¶4).

Lucky for him, as with my dream tattoo, his encounter with Green drew blood, but it did not drain life. It brought him close to death, it made him see his own mortality, with death before him in vibrant shades of green. Again, with the drawing of blood, with an act of sacrifice, the truth is revealed. The Green Knight reveals that he was the lord of the house, and the third blow was allowed to hurt for the betrayal, "for that green girdle underneath your shirt!" (Lewis, Canto 4, ¶5). What was meant to be an even trade, a just dealing, was marred, even if only slightly, by this deception and betrayal.

As we illuminated earlier, green is often associated with newness, rebirth, growth, and other positive aspects, it is full of life and endless potential. In this myth, a deadlier aspect of green is depicted, a green of challenges and life-changing choice. A green more akin to the sickly green of a poison vial or the suffocating green of an overwhelming algae bloom. These greens are fed by pride and greed, by an unconscious fertilization, the reiteration of the false promise of endless growth, and by an envious quest for power. Today, the green of the almighty dollar seems to hold the most sway.

The green dream of the Green New Deal, of a just environmental policy, activism, and the like, and the green dollar of big industry, big polluters, fossil fuel capital, battle endlessly. The green recycling arrows spin us around and around, reminding us we each have to play our role, that the die has been cast, that we must walk, lonely and scared, into the confusing landscape of monied interests. Each individual bearing the load of their carbon footprint while the corporations and industries continue forward unabated, as unkillable as the Green Knight who chuckles as he mounts his steed and carries his head away under his arm.

Perhaps the cruelest and kindest trick of the Green Knight is to make Gawain realize his imperfection and the uncertainty of his life. In the end of course, the gift and curse of the sash has all been a rouse arranged by the knight, it was as if he gifted it himself. So, on the day of the test of bravery when he nicks Gawain with the axe, he delivers the deepest blow in revealing he knows the truth of Gawain's cowardice and deceit. In the opening paragraphs of this chapter, the green fog was thick with trickery and poison, tinged by currency and exchange. It is a capitalistic bargain that we are all a part of, at least those of us who are in the "WEIRD" world of Western, educated, industrialized, rich, and democratic societies (Henrich et al., 2010).

Interestingly, in many versions of this tale, the Green Knight is not only gifted his magic by Morgan le Fey, he is also put to this task by her. She and her wyrding (ancient magic) ways are in direct contrast to the WEIRD modern world. In many of the Arthurian legends, Morgan is cast as the villainous stepsister. An outcast, bent on destroying Arthur, his knights, and most pointedly, his wife Guinevere. There is an almost irrational pale that is cast over her figure. In quite a few translations, the Green Knight is compared to the devil. Many of these tales were set in a way that valorizes the new faith (Christianity) in these parts of the world, in contrast to the old ways. In this comparison, I think the WEIRD can learn from the wyrd. There is a magic that happens when we can come together with the greening in the world, all sides of it.

In myths and tales of magic, so often the practitioner is able to perform great acts of valor, trickery, or creation seemingly from nowhere. However, when the reader digs in (and in many cases there may be an overt nod) they will find that the magic is being drawn from the natural world. These sources can be nature itself, something deep within the individual that evolved within them as a natural process, or they are gifted the power by unseen forces. All of these set the magical or wyrd outside the control of humankind and at the same time within them. This is something that is important to remember when dealing with the greening in this tale, it is not separate. We, as humans, are not outside of the green, outside of nature and the natural cycles of the world. On top of this, we are deeply rooted in it, when we recognize this connection and lean into it it is as if we are tapped into something greater than ourselves. Again, to me, this is the nature of dreams, a natural process we can access every night. These moments remind us of our dependance and co-creative power within.

With power comes responsibility, or so they say. Knowing we are connected to Earth in such a deep way can lead us to a desire to become the best stewards we can be, especially when we are trying to move toward the wyrd from the WEIRD. The truth that we need revealed lies in these vibrant shades of green, only once we each realize this interconnection and our place in nature, that we too are tied to the fate of the Earth, can we truly begin to live and grow. Once we step into this wyrding, once we face death and fate and the uncertainty of it all, perhaps we are gifted a moment of rebirth like Gawain. Once he passes his test, takes a moment to sit with the Green Knight, even laughing about all that came to pass, he feels a shift. "In his breast his heart began to sing the old, old music whose still echoes roll forever voiceless through the listening soul" (Lewis, Canto 4, ¶7). This song echoes like an incantation deep within him and in the Earth, only by humbling himself and sharing his lifeblood with the ground beneath him could he accept the gift. He had to be named imperfect and flawed, he had to be nicked by the greening blade.

We know that the Earth relies on our choices and patterns as much as we depend on her changes of seasons and weather systems. We could see this in stark detail when we locked down during the early days of the pandemic. There were abrupt shifts in direct correlation with our lightened footprint on land, sea, and air. This is a wyrding way.

Of course, this way forward does not look practical from a political or economic standpoint. We cannot remove humanities footprint, but we can make it much lighter. We have to aim for the North Star so we can hopefully fall amongst the clouds. We are imperfect in our protection of the Earth, but we need to try nevertheless. We will not recycle every plastic container, we will not reuse every bottle or bag, we may not change our lightbulbs for the more energy efficient model, or get an electric car, or go vegan. We will do only what we are able, but we must confront the problem, acknowledge the impending crisis and, most importantly, face the giant that looms. That is our true quest today.

Gawain completed his task by going into the woods, by facing and acknowledging the wyrd and WEIRD ways. He had no idea what he would find there and he fully expected to die. He went to the forest gilded in gold armor from head to toe, but he only found protection in the green of his sash, by rooting himself and giving his pride over to the wyrd ones. He had to face the uncertainty of doing things the way he was used to. He left the comfort of his WEIRD ways to venture into the green middling mess of a forest. Here the many shades are hard to differentiate, it is uncertain and fraught. We have to face this uncertain future, offer our neck to it with humility and a solid grounding. We have to grieve what has to die in us, sacrifice a vision of the future we may have had in order to see the future possibilities that lie ahead.

We believe our small rituals of sacrifice (recycling, eating less meat, whatever we choose) are the belt of our protection, but it has to be deeper and wider. Especially knowing what we know now, the many levels of deception and greed that hinder the way forward. We have to receive the cut of the axe, bleed for the cause in a metaphorical sense, tattoo our intention on our arm to be able to find our way back to the collective. Once we have received the wounding, faced the giant and recognized its power, we know we cannot go forward alone. We have to tap into that part of us that is connected to the greening of the world and carry it forward, sharing it with others. Gawain learned a form of wyrding in the grove, he marked himself with that green as we must do.

When facing climate crisis, individual rituals are important to keep us connected to the issue, a reusable bag or water bottle, can serve as a totem to connect each of us to the larger issue. Every time you make a conscious, green choice, let it serve as a touchstone, but do not let that be the end. To move forward we have to recognize our own personal failings and even more importantly, in that imperfection, shine a light on society at large, on the industries and policies that got us where we are. Lobby congress, write your representatives, hold conferences and meetups locally or virtually to cut down on travel and carbon emissions, make a plan to organize in your area of expertise, entangle yourself in climate conversation. This is such a complex issue, I hope, halfway through this text, you are starting to see where you can bring the roots and tendrils into your own life, work, creativity, or practice, in whatever imperfect way you have available to you.

Having been called out for his imperfection, Gawain must now face Arthur's court. He survived to make this return and knows he must tell his tale of bravery and cowardice. He enters a court which is "awaiting his return in anxious doubt" (Lewis, Canto 4, ¶8). His uncertainty now passed is still borne within Camelot. There is great celebration upon his return however, he knows he must confess his tale along with his imperfection and deceit. To his surprise, the full court is moved by his story. In the first edition by Kirtlan (1912/1360), rather than berating him, they decide that henceforth all the knights of the round table will wear green belts in solidarity, each knowing that they, in their cowardice, did not take up the challenge to begin with, so how could they fault him for wavering in the face of certain doom in that deep, green thicket?

From the green of death, comes the green of rebirth. As each of us confront the truth of climate crisis, we call to the larger community. We must recognize that we all fall short and, in that failure, find solidarity, humanity, and hope. We can waver in our certainty one way or the other. In life there is never one sure path forward, there is joy and pain, there are moments of calm and chaos, most of all there is uncertainty and beautiful imperfection. Just as Gawain learned, most of life is lived, fully coming to green, in the middle. We too must walk the middling way of green. We have to face all that has gone wrong to get us to this point in time: the choices that were made and those that continue to prevail in our flawed policy: the elevation of the green of capital over the green of the natural world; the scapegoating of individuals to deflect from the responsibility of these larger systems and industries.

Once we are able to confront and wade through this murky, stifling, stagnant green of death and despair, our eyes will begin to adjust. In a new light of communal purpose, wearing our green belts with pride, we can begin to see the green of change and renewal, a rebirth of a new way forward. So, is that enough on green, is green ripening for you? Is it able to find a voice of its own in your psyche and in our world today? The green path ahead will still have challenges, there will still be ambiguity in abundance, but we will not walk it alone. In our imperfection we can step forward with confidence, knowing that Green contains multitudes and only by seeing our mistakes, dying to the ways that no longer serve, and wearing our imperfection with pride, can we be an example of the change needed in the world today.

A Gray Shroud of Reflection and Connection

There is a question posed by Alice Buchanan (1932) that there was a translation error early on and that rather than green, the original Irish *glas* should be translated as "gray" (p. 327). For the purposes here, I want to hold this uncertainty and dive into it. The beauty of fairytales, legends, myths, dreams is that one does not negate the other. This green is gray too. Green and gray can be one in the same, differentiated and enlivening to one another. In Jung's (2009) *The Red Book* gray is the color for the land of death, where the "dusky, unspeakably remote horizon, where sea and sky are fused into infinity" (p. 263), all is one in this grayness.

In the introduction to Gawain and the Green Knight, Kirtlan (1912) expounds on the dreamlike quality of the tale, how the reader enters the realm of Camelot and has "mingled with the crowds at the great Feast of Pentecost, when knights and kings rode forth into green meadows" (p. 2). It puts a bit of a pallor on the realm to imagine it in the gray, rather than the green. This moves us from the livening jest of a feast into the gray death of endless horizons. This is what the Green Knight does to Gawain as well, when he walks into the court's feast at Yuletide. Interestingly, the entry in the *Dictionary of Symbols* right after green, is grey (Chevalier & Gheerbrant, 1996/1969, pp. 456–457). "Grey is the color of ashes and of mist" (p. 456). This mist, the misty, fog of uncertainty, ambiguity, sorrow, and loss. Here, the gray/green boundaries blur and the poisonous fog of green becomes the grey soot of a forest fire.

In the beginning of 2020, there were extreme forest fires happening in the Southern Hemisphere. Australia was making the news with shots of flame and smoke engulfing everything. Then, in the beginning days of the ongoing pandemic, we found ourselves in a world where an invisible virus attacks our lungs, hanging in the air along with the clarion cry of "I can't breathe." This defiant phrase echoed forth, amplifying the terrifying last words of the latest victim of our deeply flawed and racial systems in the United States, George Floyd. These images, the burning of the world (both the lungs/forests of our world through climate crisis and deforestation; as well as the burning of cities in response to political, societal unrest—with a history too long to delve into here); the stifled lungs of Pandemic victims, only able to breathe through medical intervention and in many cases artificial means of a ventilator; and finally, the complete loss of breath symbolized by George Floyd's last words, are connecting us all and crying out with a message.

In Jung's theory of synchronicity an image from the unconscious cries out (often through dreams) and is reflected in the conscious realm, reinforcing its importance for those who are able to see the deeper meaning. This was a time of intense synchronicity in our world. In dream work, where we look to our nighttime dreams for meaning and guidance, we often speak of the multi-layered nature of dreams. This refers to the fact that every dream can be viewed on not only a personal level, what that dream means to me in my life, but also what a dream may mean within my community (my family, my neighborhood, my town, etc.), or for the collective, within the world as a whole.

At the time of these protests, the pandemic, and the growing fire on our Earth, it was the season of Pentecost in the Christian faith. The symbol of the Pentecostal breath was, and I'd argue, is still reverberating on all these levels. The unconscious symbol of the inability to breathe began as a symbolic cry and has now become sadly, painfully literal. In the biblical passage on Pentecost, this breath and the blessings it bestowed were wonderous and frightening.

> When the day of Pentecost had come, the disciples were all together in one place. And suddenly from heaven there came a sound like the rush of a violent wind, and it filled the entire house where they were sitting. Divided tongues, as of fire, appeared among them, and a tongue rested on each of them. All of them were filled with the Holy Spirit and began to speak in other languages … All were amazed and perplexed, saying to one another, "What does this mean? ... Peter … raised his voice and addressed them, "… God declares, that I will pour out my Spirit upon all flesh, and your sons and your daughters shall prophesy, and your young men shall see visions, and your old men shall dream dreams. … Both men and women … I will pour out my Spirit; and they shall prophesy. And I will show portents in the heaven above and signs on the earth below, blood, and fire, and smoky mist.
>
> (New Testament KJV, Acts 2:1–19)

This breath of Pentecost gives all of humanity the ability to understand one another, to speak and be understood in one language. Will we be able to claim this amazing miracle of understanding from the fiery breath that is scorching our world today? From climate crisis, to pandemic, to systemic racism, we have deeply rooted threats that can either tear us apart or bring us together. In the smoky mist of the forest fires, the death cries, we portend the future.

We can continue to ignore the energies that are crying out to us from beloved lands, city centers, and most heartbreakingly and importantly, human voices, so often ignored in our world today. It should not take a tragic death to call our attention to this constant, deadly threat that is tied to being Black in America today. Black lives matter, each one is a gift, each one is connected inextricably to each of us. As George Floyd died, crying out for his mother, his anguished, muffled "I can't breathe" echoing the deaths of so many before him and even more after, who were taken from us due to these deeply ingrained inequalities and prejudices in our society. Many reporters at that time reported on "the dual pandemics of Covid-19 and racism," I would add to that the third layer, a third pandemic of the climate crisis, heightened by environmental injustice which is a looming threat on the edge of consciousness and threatening front-line communities. I mention this, not to detract from the pandemics at hand but to amplify them against the backdrop of yet another layer of meaning.

As I sit here writing, I try to stay deeply aware of my privilege as a white woman able to work from home during a pandemic, able to study the climate crisis from my first-world home in WEIRD America with little personal inconvenience at this time, rather than living in the chaos it is already creating in so many parts of the world. Aware that I am a white woman who does not have to worry about my children, when and if I have them, being killed just for living in the skin they were born with or to worry for myself in this way. It breaks my heart and I try to be an ally to those who are faced with these issues daily. The best way I know how to do that is to speak out, to demonstrate that I hear the cries coming from our communities of color and amplify them through my writing as best I can from my own place of privilege. I speak the names of those who have been lost to our three-fold pandemics in my heart and on the page. I feel deeply the cries of "I can't breathe" on so many levels and I weep for those lives lost and the loved ones they left behind. In this Pentecostal breath I hear the names of Elijah McClain, Ahmaud Arbery, Breanna Taylor, George Floyd, Rayshard Brooks, Ma'Khia Bryant, Tyre Nichols, and the 70 plus others from 2020 beyond on the growing memorial at Say Every Name (2023) spoken as prayer, with a fiery breath.

In depth psychology, we often discuss the concept of projection. This is the idea that whatever within me that I cannot claim for myself, I put on other people or things. On a more collective level, whatever we as society repress and ignore, will inevitably bubble up in new ways, destructive or inspiring. As I see the peaceful protests in the light of day give way to and at times corrupted by looting, burning, and violence, I know that this is the unconscious fiery breath of passion which burns once the protests fall on uncaring ears. Even though many are hearing them now, the unheard, smoldering cries are igniting after being unnoticed, with burning importance for too long. We are seeing these scenes of cities burning, these fires sparked from the last breath that escaped Floyd's burning lungs and we can respond in one of two ways.

We, as members of a society that allows racism to run rampant, who do not administer equal healthcare and human rights to every member of our community, who let the world burn and ignore the teachings of science which can guide us, can either ignore the cry to change and carry on unheeded. Or we can use this time to emblazon our resolve to change, to light the fires within ourselves, to brandish our green sash of courage into the grey smog of loss and pain. We can view these scenes of unrest with an empathetic eye and understand that so many are hurting in our world today. The issues that the news channels are reporting now, and that this viral pandemic of COVID-19 brought to light, are not new. So many are without: without safety daily, without healthcare, without sufficient income, without food, without shelter, without justice, without equality, without freedom, without their voices being heard. So, before you condemn those who you do not understand, those actions that make you uncomfortable, and those fires that seem to speak more loudly than the dying cries of yet another Black life, take a moment, and breathe.

Breathe in a prayer and breathe out their names. Breathe in the realization of your privilege, those who are in that position, and breathe out a commitment to speak out, to be an ally, to vote for change, to call out the problems in our broken system. Breathe with your hopefully healthy lungs and breathe out a healing breath to all those who are struggling to do so on their own, those who are currently suffering respiratory illness and those with disabilities that place them at even higher risk. Breathe in the fresh air you take for granted, be that through a mask, thanks to clean air from a purifier, or from any small patch of green you can find and breathe out the resolve to make a better planet for seven generations beyond yourself.

Finally, breathe in a new vision of the future and breathe out your memory of the past. We are in a time where we cannot go back, we cannot be comfortable with how things have been, we must move forward knowing it will be uncomfortable, uncertain. In our discomfort, comes necessary change. It is never an easy task to become more than we have been, to dig deeply into our own biases and prejudices, to realize that the lives we live are vastly different than others our society is so used to ignoring. But only by doing this, by recognizing who we are, our imperfections, our biases, our prejudice, our privilege, and where we fall short, can we see the truth of others. When we see these things in ourselves, we can lift the fog and start to view others without projecting our poisons on them.

This is the Pentecostal spirit, it burns, and it confounds, but most importantly, as we see in the passage above, it gives the gift of connection and prophesy. Once we brave the possibility of getting burned (or like Gawain, sacrifice ourselves for a greater story), put ourselves out there to be an ally and advocate for the needed changes to our systems and planet, only then can we understand one another and see all that the future could offer. So, as we "say their names" and cry out "I can't breathe," remember why we say these words. Feel each letter as it crosses your lips, feel the air flow across your tongue, feel the heat rise as it dances down your throat and into your chest.

As it rests in your lungs, feel it press against your heart, with each beat growing warmer and warmer. Now, know that these words are a righteous fire, a prayer for the future. Let them burn in you, let them burn down all those former viewpoints that no longer serve us or our systems, let these systems burn and know what a world can look like if we imagine them anew; and now, speak out with conviction, say his name, say their names, say her name; make a change; breathe in love and breathe out hope. And in this final breath, feel the heat of the fire of a world forever changed and know that, on this symbolic level, you too must let the words "I can't breathe" burn you down before you can rebuild.

Fires of Change

In the *Dictionary of Symbols* (Chevalier & Gheerbrant, 1996/1969) green is inextricably linked to red. In many descriptions there, red and green are two sides of the same being, or they hold the energy of one within or in contrast to the other. Many of these connections suggest that one cannot have green without red (pp. 451–456). When I think of green it calls to mind nature, trees, plants, the flora of the Earth. But green is also "the colour of water, as red is the colour of fire" (p. 451). Those blue-green waters, cooling and calming, pull in their fiery opposite, an element that demands sacrifice.

Fire is placed into the elemental quaternity with water, earth, and air, but of all these, "fire is the odd one out. It synthesizes its surroundings, takes its character from its context ... It's a shapeshifter" (Pyne, 2015). Here is the tricky Knight again, shapeshifting and demanding his cut. In fact, throughout *Gawain and the Green Knight,* there are very few colors mentioned, the only other, in regard to the knight, is red. He has red eyes (Kirtlan, 1912/1360, p. 79). Since one's eyes are the window to the soul, indeed, here there is red deep within this green.

In the natural world, and in some indigenous myths, there is also an innate red within green. In the Nimíipuu culture (also referred to as the Nez Percé, located in what is now known as the Pacific Northwest region of the United States) "the pine-trees had the secret of fire, and guarded it jealously from the rest of the world" (Rubens, J. as cited by R. L. Packard, 1891, p. 327). This tale, titled "How Beaver stole Fire from the Pines" goes on to recall how beaver, secreting a coal in his breast, outran all the pines and a ceder, leaving them on the banks of rivers and on hills. Eventually, he began giving fire to other trees, willow, birch, "and so on to certain other kinds of wood. Since then, all who have wanted fire have got it from these particular woods, because they have fire in them" (p. 328). This is the red within the green, released by friction when two pieces of said wood are rubbed together "in the manner of the 'old timers'" (p. 329; Figure 4).

Figure 4 Drawing, *Rooted in Fire and Smoke*, colored pens and markers on paper, by the author.

Though fire is a part of nature and the natural process, it comes in both a creative and destructive form. Once Homo Sapiens began to control fire, we had a tendency to lean into the worst of its qualities and the power it granted to slip outside the bounds of natural constraints. In an essay that dives deeply into this realm of fire, Professor Stephen J. Pyne (2015) reminds us that "fire takes apart what photosynthesis puts together." Red and green pitted against one another, and yet, reliant on their opposite. As mentioned above, fire "synthesizes its surroundings" (Pyne, 2015), it is deeply relational: it relies on a fuel source, oxygen, and optimal conditions to grow and spread.

Once, that fuel source was largely wood based. As industrialization increased, especially in our WEIRD societies, we had to reach "into the deep past and [exhume] lithic landscapes," we "removed open flame, simplified it into chemical combustion, and stuffed it into chambers" (Pyne, 2015). The more we grew our relationship with fire, the more we were able to step away from the rest of the natural world. We found we could keep warm in winter, we could dry things in a storm, we could read well into the night. All the usual constraints placed on other beings by natural cycles, weather conditions, and even time, no longer held us back.

With further confining and combustion, we found we could travel long distances, even into outer space, even gravity was no match for the force of "plumes of flame" (Pyne, 2015). We remade our place on the planet in its image, burning down anything that did not suit us with an almost unsatiable hunger, like a wildfire with unlimited fuel. Pyne (2015) stated that the term Anthropocene, the new epoch we find ourselves in, "might equally be called the Pyrocene." We are reshaping the world in its image, melting the ice sheets, warming the oceans, leaving burned and dried landscapes in our wake.

Fire has given us it's power, it has also given us firepower and firearms in the lethality of the gun, missiles, bombs, and other weapons of war and hate. This fire is not held in the heart and passed on to others with a sense of care and justice, as Beaver illustrated. This fire is held at arm's length, a removed, remote, empowering extension of our dominant humanity. With this fire we hold life and death in our hands or in the touch of a button, or flick of a switch. With modern weapons of war, a drone operator can kill hundreds without ever leaving the confines of their room. This fire removed us even further from the patterns and connections of life and nature. This fire is the red of death.

In the tale of Gawain, this fire is found in the drawing of blood and the immediacy of the Green Knight who's "horse's hoofs struck fire from the flinty stones" of the hall as he turned to leave (pp. 80–81), the promise of certain fate ringing behind him in the court. This is not a Pentecostal fire, burning within, connecting and uniting us. This is the fire of rage and the pain of injustice that sparks riots and angry counter protests. Smoke from this fire leaves us gasping for breath and in a fog of war.

In February of 2024, as the world watched the fourth month of the recent and ongoing conflict between Palestine and Israel, fire meets with fire on multiple levels. Just as the smoke and fire in the reflection above, in lungs yearning for breath move us into a new vision of justice and equity. This fire, one of self-immolation, should move us back to the fire of creation rather than destruction.

On Sunday February 25, Arron Bushnell was the second American to light themselves on fire in service to the ongoing calls for cease-fire. This type of protest is extreme and heartbreaking. Bushnell was an American service member one of those who "profess to be willing to give up their lives for whatever the U.S. politicians or government decide is best for another country—'freedom and democracy'" (Wright, 2024). In his last words, Bushnell decried his country's role in the ongoing conflict, stated that he was "about to engage in an extreme act of protest" (as cited by Veterans for Peace, 2024), and set himself alight to emblazon his message on the world.

This sacrificial fire is not an anomaly, there have been individuals all over the world who have self-immolated to spark a conversation, a movement, with the hopes of much needed change. In 2010, the Arab Spring caught fire because of the Tunisian street vendor Mohamed Bouazizi, an act which "sparked citizen throughout the Middle East to challenge their repressive governments" (Wright, 2024). When I was living in Washington, DC in 2013, there was another incident of this on the National Mall, I remember being struck by this extreme act only miles from where we lived at the time. I followed up to learn more, but never could find an answer, cause, or cry of protest to connect to this incident, it remains in my mind, ambiguous and mournful.

A mere five years later another man, David Buckel, did the same in New York's Prospect Park. In his note to the *New York Times*, he stated, "my early death from fossil fuels reflects what we are doing to ourselves" and that he wanted to serve "an honorable purpose in death" (Buckel as cited in Mays, 2018). He stated that many were dying early from polluted air, water, soil, and the growing inhabitability of the planet. You can see in his words that fire, in this act of self-sacrifice, is lit for a greater good, the hopes for the world elevated above a single life. One can only imagine that these individuals had a fire burning within them. During the Vietnam War, Martin Luther King, Jr. (1967) reminded an audience at Riverside Church in Manhattan, that at this time "the words of John F. Kennedy come back to haunt us … 'Those who make peaceful revolutions impossible will make violent revolution inevitable'" (p. 6).

From that time to the current conflicts, to the climate crisis, a revolution is boiling under the currents of these crises, fire that cannot be contained, was made literal, spilling outward, consuming. As US Airman Aaron Bushnell burned alive, crying out, one officer came to his aid while another pointed his gun at Aaron. Fires of desperation cannot be put out by fires of destruction. The mention of this is not to glamorize this extreme action, but rather to look at it from a perspective of understanding and depth. If nothing else, seeing this should make us wonder what could light a fire within us, rather than without. This is the fire needed in these times. We need a creative, lifegiving, fire, a fire of warmth, love, understanding and compassion to counter those destructive, violent flames. We need fiery action and compassionate, revolutionary care and concern. We need an uprising that lights hearts and minds on fire with action and hope for change.

Protest is an issue that is intimately connected to the climate, culture, and politics. It is also an act that can be deeply psychological. Most protests that we hear about are far less extreme than the tragic incidents above, however, they hold a fire all their own. In the protests after George Floyd was killed, we could see this fire burning. In the years before and since, these fiery outcries have been for #MeToo, women's rights, civil rights, LGBTQIA+ rights, and the climate. Each one may be unique and passionate, but they all seek to stoke the fires, to burn away injustice and create the world anew. In MLK's words above we can hear the jovial call of the Green Knight. If Gawain had come to his fate honestly, and with a brave heart, his blood wouldn't have been spilt. Similarly, if those who are in power can come to hear the cries of protest over all these issues, issues that are interconnected at a deep and poignant level: climate crisis, war, pandemic, civil rights, human rights, justice, and equity perhaps we can avoid the worst of what is ahead.

All of these aspirations for our world require a vision that plunges us into the fiery truth of the world around us. We need to find heart even in the clutches of money and power. The business-as-usual policies increasingly put profits over people, they wrap the blood that is spilled daily in the shroud of green capital. They burn the greens of renewal and care that could be invested in health into a fiery, feverish return to "normal." They trade the green of nature for the scorching promise of endless growth. These arsonists "go around the globe setting fires faster than we can extinguish them … [profiting] from death and suffering" (Veterans for Peace, 2024). All of Earth's beauty and humanity is seemingly fodder for these powerbroker's blazing greed, all viewed simply as collateral damage. We need a new green and red of renewal to fight these fires and transmute them.

In the Arthurian legends, one of the most well-known tropes is that of the Grail. This cup is a sacred and revitalizing vessel. It is the spark for many quests and contains an air of mystery. The grail is said to hold the blood of Christ, interpretations and modern retellings vary on how literal this quality is. Of course, in this context, we will lean into the both/and. This grail is "a vessel of emerald or green crystal … which holds the blood … In it, coalesce all those notions of love and sacrifice which condition the regeneration … in which dawn and dusk, death and rebirth come together and strike a balance" (Chevalier & Gheerbrant, 1969/1996, p. 455). Red within green, a fire of sacrifice and love held gently within a promise of renewal and redemption.

One of the most striking protest movements in recent years is that of Extinction Rebellion (XR). This group, most often seen clad in red robes or dresses, with their faces painted white, are a beautifully poignant and artistic movement. Though it seems in recent years that their numbers and appearances have dwindled, the visual shock, if you have ever seen them, is sure to light a fire of wonder within. This is the place where I think protest can be extremely effective, by sparking debate and conversation.

Over the past two to three years, there has been an increasing number of protests in spaces of highly cultural value, specifically art museums. Many of these have been in WEIRD nations, from Europe, to Australia, to Canada, and the United States, though I am sure there are many I have missed that fall outside of these regions. One thing has connected them all, climate protest. In these shocking moments, protesters who seem like fellow patrons, admiring a piece of art, suddenly toss liquid on the artwork, paint, soup (both tomato and pea), mashed potatoes, black goo, etc. Then, unveiling banners, T-shirts with messages, shouting words of protest, and sometimes glueing themselves to the wall, floor, or frames they state their grievance. There is an element of performance in these moments.

They light a fire under the movement for climate change, if only for a moment. On social media the comments on these articles are wide and varied. To some, they are heroes, to others, villains. Many don't understand why throwing food on a cultural treasure is appropriate or effective. In my view, the fact that people are wondering this is exactly the point, it is opening a portal for them into the uncertainty of it all. Rarely has an artwork been damaged in any significant way, they are usually well protected by glass. But even if they were, this is surely a damage that can be repaired, right? Who is to say. And again, this is the point.

If we are willing to step so far over the edge in service to the fires of progress, we must live with the uncertainty and ambiguity the future will hold. To protest is to care. To light oneself on fire with the burning hope of change. These smaller, less extreme acts of protest can still have a similar effect to deadly acts of sacrifice. In these small moves we show how we put human life, in the form of our cultural treasures, above all else. People typically view the destruction of a piece of art as more devastating than the death of an ecosystem. I am certainly not intending to demean great works of art, as a daughter of two art majors, I have a healthy and long-formed love of arts and crafts. This is the power of these small moments of protest. They make us question our values, they put things in perspective. Just like a piece of art does for each person who views it.

Cultural products are of high value because they are so subjective. A line in a poem, a passage from a book, a painting, or a sculpture holds multitudes. It holds history and beauty, wisdom and mystery, each new age views the artwork of the past in a new light, learning something about the time before, but, maybe most importantly, what it has to say to the present moment. If you haven't caught on already, this is the culture that I have been trying to infuse into each chapter through verse and image. Though my artwork is by no means a masterpiece, I hope it serves to move you in one way or another. These are my musings in image form, each stroke and scratch connected me more deeply to the topic at hand and I hope they do the same for you.

Art is a great connector. It lives in the middle, a product of green, renewal, and death in one. The red lives here as well. Just as it does in the fires of protest when artwork is targeted as a means to an end. The uncertainty in these acts, not the act itself, that is quite definite and certain, but rather, the uncertainty in the emotion it will provoke and the ambiguity of damage and possibility for repair. This is the same place we find ourselves in the climate crisis, uncertain of recovery, mitigation, or adaptation, what it will look like and who will be served by it.

One of the last notes I will throw onto this fire of inquiry is the natural regenerative quality of fire, one I think we can all benefit from today. There are certain plants which are classified as *pyrophytes* and *pyrophiles*. The former are plants which are extremely well adapted to fire, they have thick bark or moist tissue that insulates them, they have sprouts that quickly grow from any scarred surface, or they have adapted to branch only high up, so that precious seeds and growth remain out of reach. The latter, the *pyrophiles*, need fire, they even produce sap that encourages it. There are some types of plants in this category whose seeds will not sprout without fire. The seed, such as the lodgepole pine … are completely sealed with resin" so they "can only open to release their seeds after the heat of a fire has physically melted [it]" (Petruzzello, 2014), the holders of fire, pine, reliant on that same force to grow anew.

This indigenous space of fire resistance and resilience can light the path ahead. Instead of being burned by the all-consuming fire of power and greed, we can grow out of its destruction with our own flames alight. From this place of renewal, we must learn to put out the fires that threaten our very exitance. These existential fires require a different kind of firefight. Not one of guns and bombs, one that does not ignore collateral damage. Rather, this one weeps for all that was lost and becomes emblazoned with a passion for others and Earth. "Fire prevention in this context means prohibiting the lobbying, advertising, vote buying, campaign funding, and actual legislation writing that corporations do behind constitutional shields" (Veterans for Peace, 2024). Preventing these fires places people over profits. Engaged citizenship, peaceful protest, works of art, and cultural movements are just a few ways to spark a movement to fight their destructive firepower. We need to light fires of our own, of heart, love, care, equity, justice, and peace.

These fires are lifegiving. They renew and bring forth the next generation. This is the red that is also green. The green that lets us know that Spring is near, small leaves and buds poking out of the grey winter. The green of life shining out from the *glas* of death (the green/grey). In this space, green and grey and red are all one, they move effortlessly between one another, middling, uncertain, ambiguous, but always burning forward. They acknowledge the loss in the world, loss of habitable climate, death of war and pandemic, the destructive pollutants environmentally, culturally, socially, and politically. They drag us into the depths of the earth and demand a sacrifice. As we see the blood of our imperfection and uncertainty light upon the snow, let it root there, a fire growing inside, to blossom, red from green, proclaiming its mark on the green Earth.

Resources

Allen, D., Linsley, C., Johl, A., & Spoelman, N. (2024). *The fraud of plastic recycling*. The Center for Climate Integrity. https://climateintegrity.org/plastics-fraud

Buchanan, A. (1932). The Irish framework of Sir Gawain and the Green Knight. In *Publications of the Modern Language Association of America, 47*(2) (pp. 315–338).

Chevalier, J., & Gheerbrant, A. (1996). *Dictionary of symbols* (J. Buchanan-Brown, Trans.). Penguin Books. (Original work published 1969.)

Henrich, J., Heine, S., & Norenzayan, A. (2010). The weirdest people in the world? In *Behavioural and Brain Sciences 33*(2/3) (pp. 61–83).

Jimison, R. (2017). *Why we all need green in our lives*. CNN Health. https://www.cnn.com/2017/06/05/health/colorscope-green-environment-calm/index.html

Jung, C. G., & Shamdasani, S. (2009). *The red book: Liber novus* (Readers ed.). (S. Shamdasani, Ed.). Norton.

King, M. L. (1967). *Beyond Vietnam: A time to break silence* [Talk]. https://www2.hawaii.edu/~freeman/courses/phil100/17.%20MLK%20Beyond%20Vietnam.pdf

Kirtlan, E. J. (Trans.). (1912). *Sir Gawain and the green knight*. Charles H. Kelly. (Original work published 1360). https://www.google.com/books/edition/Sir_Gawain_and_the_Green_Knight/hE-PkaijRBIC?hl=en&gbpv=1&pg=PP11&printsec=

Lewis, C. M. (1903). *Gawayne and the Green Knight: A fairy tale*. Yale University Press. https://www.gutenberg.org/ebooks/14410

Mays, J. C. (2018, April 14). Prominent lawyer in fight for gay rights dies after setting himself on fire in Prospect Park. *New York Times*. https://www.nytimes.com/2018/04/14/nyregion/david-buckel-dead-fire.html

Packard, R. L. (1891). Notes on the mythology and religion of the Nez Perces. In *The Journal of American Folklore*, *4*(15) (pp. 327–330). https://www.jstor.org/stable/pdf/533388.pdf

Petruzzello, M. (2014, April 7). Playing with wildfire: 5 amazing adaptations of pyrophytic plants. *Encyclopedia Britannica*. https://www.britannica.com/list/5-amazing-adaptations-of-pyrophytic-plants

Pyne, S. J. (2015, May 5). The fire age. *Aeon*. https://aeon.co/essays/how-humans-made-fire-and-fire-made-us-human

Say Every Name (2023) *#Say their names* [List All-Photos]. Sayevery.name. https://sayevery.name/

Taylor, J. (1998). *The living labyrinth: Exploring universal themes in myth, dreams, and the symbolism of waking life*. Paulist Press.

ter Halle, A., & Ghiglione, J. F. (2021). Nanoplastics: A complex, polluting terra incognita. In *Environmental Science and Technology, 55*(21) (pp. 14466–14469). Retrieved from https://pubs.acs.org/doi/10.1021/acs.est.1c04142

Veterans for Peace. (2024, February 27). Aaron Bushnell is the latest victim of madmen arsonists [Opinion]. *Common Dreams*. https://www.commondreams.org/opinion/aaron-bushnell-gaza-free-palestine

Wright, A. (2024, February 26). Why would anyone kill themselves to stop a war? On Aaron Bushnell and others [Opinion]. *Common Dreams*. https://www.commondreams.org/opinion/kill-selves-to-stop-war

4 Tears from the Melting Ice

Monumental Loss

In August of 2019, *Okjokull*, the "Ok Glacier" in Iceland lost its glacial status. Approximately five years prior, glaciologist Oddur Sigurdsson pronounced Ok's death. When a glacier loses enough mass that it ceases to move, when there is not enough snow coming down to revitalize it and pack together in any meaningful way "We call that dead ice," Sigurdsson stated (cited in Luckhurst, 2019). He noticed that the snow had been melting prior to any accumulation on the surface of Ok since 2003 (via satellite images). Despite the visibility of the ice body to the popular tourist attraction and well used Ring Road nearby, the death of this glacier was announced to very little fanfare (Luckhurst, 2019).

In order to make this issue more visible, a group of academics, scientists, and artists came together to create a film "Not Ok" (2018) and to create a memorial plaque to the lost figure. Anthropologist Dominic Boyer noted that plaques are often used to mark human accomplishments or notable events. Where I live, in Virginia, USA, I see plaques to the Revolutionary and Civil War wins and losses all over the countryside. Just up the road, in Washington, DC, similarly, monuments stand to past presidents, Martin Luther King, Jr., and a myriad of dead from World War I and beyond. Plaques litter the streets naming people and places where historic events occurred, many of whom are replicated in granite just a short walk away. Dr. Boyer said that for this reason a plaque seemed fitting as "The passing of a glacier is also a human accomplishment … in that it is anthropogenic climate change that drove this" (cited in Luckhurst, 2019). The plaque was written by Icelandic author Andri Snaer Magnason (2019) and states in Icelandic and English:

> A letter to the future
> Ok is the first Icelandic glacier to lose its status as a glacier.
> In the next 200 years all our glaciers are expected to follow the same path.
> This monument is to acknowledge that we know

DOI: 10.4324/9781032644820-5

what is happening and what needs to be done.
Only you know if we did it.
August 2019
415ppm CO_2

This is a beautiful and striking example of recognizing the ambiguous loss we are all facing. In 200 years, "only you know if we did it," you being of the uncertain future. The film and plaque became much more widely noticed than the initial announcement of the bare data and fact of the glaciers' demise. It took creativity and communal action to bring it into widespread public consciousness. When I first heard about this, I was struck not only by the simple beauty of the act, but also by the revolutionary shift it made.

Plaques are placed for acts of humanity, but monuments are placed for extraordinary beings. It may be a small plaque, but it reads "this monument." Monuments are placed in remembrance of people. Certainly, this may be a translation issue and it also holds the meaning of the chosen word, both/and. There is always something lost in translation, but perhaps here, something is also gained. Ok is personified in this small move. In the opening chapters, I noted my affinity for ice, they have become a dear friend, I mourn their loss daily, pieces being chipped away by the figurative fires of our warming planet. In this one word, perhaps others can find the space and importance to mourn them too.

There has been a movement for over 50 years to give rights of personhood to nature. In 1972, a professor at the University of Southern California published a law review article on this topic. Less than a year later the Supreme Court in the United States had a case that put this to the test *Sierra Club v. Morton*. Unfortunately, the suit was rejected, but in his dissent, Justice William O. Douglas (1972) wrote that if a corporation is a "'person' for purposes of the adjudicatory processes … So it should be as respects valleys, alpine meadows, rivers, lakes, estuaries, beaches, ridges, groves of trees, swampland, or even air that feels the destructive pressure of modern technology and modern life" (p. 405, U.S. 745). There are a number of countries and municipalities who seemingly agree with this opinion and the rights of nature movement has been making its way through the courts and even into law ever since.

In 2008, Ecuador became the first country to enshrine this vision into their constitution. Nevertheless in 2021, communities near Los Cedros, an incredibly biodiverse cloud forest, had to bring a lawsuit to protect the area from mining (Greenfield, 2021). Thankfully, they won that suit and the landmark ruling extended the rights of nature to "the whole country, not just to protected areas" (Greenfield, 2021). In Bangladesh, legal protection to all rivers was granted in 2019. Activists there hoped to "give the environment a more central place in humanity's expanding moral circle—the imaginary boundary we draw around those we consider worthy of moral consideration" (Samuel, 2019). This was a monumental leap in that it granted rights to more than a singular body of water or particular landscape, all rivers are now protected. From New Zealand to parts of the Amazon in Brazil, granting personhood to rivers have had in impact on law, hope, and the spirit of conservation, especially for Indigenous communities who call these areas home (Maisonnave et al., 2023; Perry, 2022).

There are many more examples that could be added here, the movement is growing and gaining traction in many parts of the world, especially in the courts. This may seem a bit removed from politics, but often, when politics fail, the court has to pick up the slack. When things are not enshrined in law, and even when they are, like in Ecuador, the courts have to play a role. (This is not to say that courts cannot or are not political, judges are appointed by or elected under the political auspices of a certain party. Nevertheless, ideally, they make decisions divorced from political influence and that is what we will lean into here, while holding the knowledge, the ambiguity of where this ideal is confronted by reality.)

This brings us full circle, back to the first chapter. The doom of the environmental crisis we find ourselves engulfed in. This doom is pitted against the just ruling of courts, the dōm, statute, or judgment that in these cases have preserved natural spaces for future generations. Fairly recently, a high court in India even invoked "*parens patriae* jurisdiction" wherein the government is required to "act as a guardian to those who cannot care for themselves" (Surma, 2022). Justice Srimthy even made a point of assigning the state responsibility to "take appropriate steps to protect Mother Nature in all possible ways" (Surma, 2022). This decision was one of many high court decisions around India "recognizing that glaciers, rivers, animals and Mother Earth have legal personhood status" (Surma, 2022).

As with so many policies and decisions we have discussed so far, the other side of doom comes into play, that of an uncertain fate. While these decisions in India are binding within states, they are not on a federal level. In the United States, more than 30 states or municipalities have made similar moves, again, the federal view of these is precarious. Policy is only as good as the systems in place that can reinforce it. It is only stable as long as the incentives that back it can outweigh, out-pay, or outplay those who put them at risk. This is by no means meant to downplay the significance of these rulings. They are monumental moves and I sincerely hope they last similarly, marking these points in time as a beacon to the future. If nothing else, they have shown us another way to look at nature and all the elements of our planet that are currently at risk.

These ideas of personhood for nature are a legal reframing, but one that could lead to a shift in the way we imagine nature and Earth themselves. In many myths, Earth is created from the bones of giants or gods. In Norse mythology, the myths of the people of Iceland, where Okjokull was memorialized, the whole of Midgard, Earth, was created in this fashion. In the *Prose Edda* we see the creation of earth from the body of a titan-like being, Ymir.

Figure 5 Drawing, *Blood from a Glacier,* colored pens and markers on paper, by the author.

The god Odin and his brothers gave Ymir a fatal wound, "from his blood they made the seas and lakes." They then fashioned Earth "from the flesh, and a mountain cliff from the bones. They made stones and gravel from the teeth," finally, they "took his skull and from it made thereof the sky. They raised it over the earth" and thus the world was complete (Sturluson, 2005, p. 16). Flesh, bones, and blood, the celestial and material made one. The earth was given new life from the remains of the dead. It is a permanent marker of the titan that was overcome (Figure 5).

A Cathedral of Time

In the mythology of Ymir, Odin, and the creation of the Earth, there is no particular timeline listed. In the Christian bible, the world and all its surrounds are created in seven days. In many other myths and legends, these massive acts of creation happen in moments, some springing into existence fully formed. In the life of our Earth, unfortunately this process took infinitely longer and to remake it seems unimaginable. To reframe the idea of nature or natural processes took, as we saw, close to 50 years and is still unformed. Of course, these ideas have been around far longer, especially in Indigenous culture and religion, this was never a question. However, to build a viable system of law or policy around it, especially in WEIRD countries, is a towering task.

I'm sure many remember when the iconic Notre Dame Cathedral was burning in Paris in April of 2019. I recall this image all over social media and on the news, as well as the distress and grief that many felt. In quite a few environmentally minded groups around that time, I heard critiques voiced that this manufactured cultural structure was sadly drawing more outrage than the burning of our planet. Around that time and on into the same year, the Amazon, "the lungs of the world" were burning, California and other parts of the United States were ablaze, and of course, Australia experienced terrible fires the following year. As the next few years passed, it seemed none of these awful events went as viral as the accidental destruction of Notre Dame.

Both are devastating losses, one of the natural world and the other of our human cultural heritage. Afterward, Notre Dame's flames were quenched, big-money donors came out of the woodworks, and a process of restoration and rebuilding began immediately. Sadly, our natural world is still on fire. The Amazon continues to burn off and on each year. In 2023, the smoke of forest fires in the high Canadian north, in boreal forests, another lung on our planet, began to sting the eyes of Americans and Canadians all across these countries. In a strange mirroring of those who watched Notre Dame burn. "Those looking on as flames engulf the building are in tears. Their dismay is shared by believers and non-believers alike in a nation where faith has long ceased to be a binding force" (Astier, 2019). All of a sudden, if only for a moment, everyone was united in their discomfort. The smoke of the fires seemed to lift a veil on the fire that is burning our world.

Though not as dramatic or moving to most, there are cathedrals burning down every day in the icy realms of our planet. From 2022 to 2023, the Greenland ice sheet has lost an average of 270 billion metric tons of ice per year. This has contributed to sea level rise since it is land-based ice. (The easiest way to think about and discern the effect of ice melt of land bound ice vs. sea or water-based ice is by imagining a glass of water with ice cubes in it. When the ice melts, the water levels don't change. However, if you were to add new ice cubes to the glass it would overflow, sea levels rise.) In satellite images compiled into a time-lapse of Greenland, with an orange and red hanging over the image indicating ice mass changes, wide edges of the country look as if they have been badly scorched (NASA & JPL/Caltech, 2023) only a small central area to the north is still depicted in white.

In this video illustration, the dramatic coloration of the edges of Greenland, the orange and red creeping ever inward, take place in seconds, but represent over 20 years. Even so, this is a massive increase in ice melt from the prior 100 years or more. The big ice that we see today is generally a remnant from the last ice age, between 26 and 19 thousand years ago. In that time, the ice has receded at a glacial pace. Now, "glacial pace" perhaps has a less momentous feel, given we may all see more glaciers, beyond Okjokull pass in our lifetime. Though we need solutions that will make adaptation possible on a quicker time scale, I think we need a broader view to address this problem. One that leans into the towering weight of what lies before us, one that honors the age of ice and the cathedrals of blue that are melting away every day.

Anthony Leiserowitz, director of the Yale Program on Climate Change Communication, said "The climate needs big, public, audacious goals that everyone can contribute to." He also noted that "Cathedrals were not completed in the lifetime of anyone starting them, but communities bought into these projects" (as cited in Coren, 2023). These he appropriately termed "cathedral projects." The idea behind them would be similar to what was presented by the idea of a Green New Deal in the United States' progressive politics, large ranging and interconnected projects. These would take climate into account in every decision, infrastructure would be made "green," technologies would build toward a carbon neutral future, cities and towns would restructure in accordance with climate goals, these would be massive leaps into our uncertain future.

On a worldwide level, goals would include rebuilding coral reefs, reforesting, restructuring, whatever you can imagine, throw it into the mix, no idea is too lofty. Leiserowitz commented that these should be bold and "transcendent projects for the collective good that encompass generations" (as cited in Coren, 2023). Looking into the history of cathedral building is fascinating and so far removed from what industry and economy implements today. These were structures that were built to last. They pulled knowledge from centuries before building their impressive monuments to something greater than themselves. They could take decades or even centuries to complete, those who worked on them, both skilled and unskilled laborers, were brought together in a communal effort, one few "expected to see finished during their lifetimes" (Durham World Heritage Site, 2024). Rather, it was an opportunity "to be part of a process that was larger than oneself" (Durham World Heritage Site, 2024).

Projects that are tangled in any goal to address the ever-growing climate catastrophe must be equally complex and vast. Given everything that's already been touched on here, we begin to grasp the hyperobject that is global warming. We need a similarly towering and elaborate goal. Unfortunately, "for governments and companies" decision-making is extremely "truncated by election cycles and quarterly earnings reports" (Coren, 2023). This is not a business-as-usual problem, it cannot be compressed in the fast-flowing world of capitalist earnings and financial gains. We need to slow the flow down. Though many effects of global warming are "already essentially irreversible," like "ocean acidification, melting ice, and some sea level rise" (Coren, 2023), it doesn't mean in setting these long-term goals, they can't have some more immediate effects.

Cathedral projects can bring communities together with a common goal, they can lift spirits, give spaces to connect, grieve, imagine, and plan. When they were building cathedrals in the Middle Ages, they remembered the ways of the past and imagined into the future. This is what we need at this moment. At the base of a glacier, you can imagine what it must have looked like, years or decades before, you can also plan for a future where less loss may be possible. On the surface of glaciers and ice sheets we can see the both/and, we feel the loss and we are enlivened by hope. There is a feeling, looking at the pocked surface of the melting glaciers in our world today that make space for the monumental. The largess of them makes them otherworldly while they are firmly rooted in the immediacy of the now.

In 1986, a large iceberg calved (split off) from an ice shelf in Antarctica. It remained embedded against the sea floor for over 15 years before it started to journey again. In 2020 Iceberg A23a began floating slowly around the Antarctic coast. By January of 2024 it was moving past the tip of the peninsula. On January 14, an expedition with a photographer and videographer were able to capture the tabular (flat topped) berg. As the tides licked its surface and winds whipped its sides, massive archways and caves were forming. The bright blue where the surface was being washed away created stunning images as strikingly beautiful and architectural as any cathedral. The videographer, Richard Sidey hints at the enormity of it "I don't think we can fathom just how big it is; we can only know how big it is from science" (as cited in Amos, 2024). In his words I hear the echoes of the hyperobject and of the uncertainty we face tackling such big problems, it is a cathedral project all its own.

As beautiful as these ocean worn structures are, they are a sign of decay. The moment the iceberg calved, it started its life anew, a life destined to end. There will never be a plaque commemorating A23a, it is its own monument. It will probably be forgotten as it slowly slips into the salty waters. As it melts away, it becomes a cathedral of mourning. It is a symbol of all that climate is doing to these vast ice bodies, the heat slowly, but surely, burning them away into obscurity. Unlike cathedrals of wood and stone, these cannot be rebuilt. This iceberg will never be seen again, aside from photographs, video, or scientific data and charts. When they burn down, there is nothing we can do, no wealthy donors to step in. As the icebergs dissolve, glaciers, ice caps, and ice sheets melt, they return to the realm of Sedna, intricately entangled in the mother of the sea's grasp.

Dreaming Bones

As the blue bones of the iceberg are revealed and it returns to the deep ocean, Sedna rises to the surface. Caught in a fisherman's net, she is unknown and unrecognized. She strikes fear into his heart and after so many years under the water, she has decayed too. Unlike the blue ice, Sedna, as Skeleton Woman is as white as the snow and stripped bare. This version of Sedna is seen in Clarissa Pinkola-Estes' *Women Who Run with Wolves* (1997). After she finds herself accidentally towed into the snowhouse of the fisherman. After a moment, "thank the Gods, thank Raven, yes, and all bountiful Sedna, safe … at … last" (p. 137), he collects himself and the fear abates.

Sedna and Skeleton Woman are different and yet the same. Here, she is the god in disguise, a common trope in mythology. Often one small kindness is given so the truth can be revealed. In many of these types of tales, a wish is granted as well. Here, in this story, Sedna, Skeleton Woman, is also Lady Death. "Lady Death is not graciously granting any wishes" (p. 146) instead she clings and demands, she becomes entangled in our lives. "For without her, there can be no real knowledge of life … or love" (p. 146) instead, she demands us to go the distance.

Once the distance was run and they are settled together in the snowhouse, despite his reticence, "some kindness came into his breathing" (p. 146) and slowly he begins to untangle her from his net. Well into the night he works, patiently and dedicated, he moves over her body untangling her. Finally, he wraps her in furs to warm her and he eventually falls asleep. "Soon [he] was dreaming. And sometimes as humans sleep, you know, a tear escapes from the dreamer's eye" (p. 138) maybe it was "a dream of sadness or longing" who is to say? Skeleton Woman saw the tear like a beacon in the dark. She was so thirsty she began to drink and "the single tear became a river and she drank and drank and drank" (p. 138).

As she lay by him drinking, she heard his heart drumming away. She took his heart out, held it in her hand, and it drummed her back to life. She sang with the beating of his heart and as she sang, her flesh and hair returned, she was renewed, alive and whole. She and the fisherman, skin to skin, awoke "wrapped around one another, tangled … in another way now, a good and lasting way" (p. 138). The only way to get to this place was through kindness and compassion, he was able to breathe his way into her heart and she in turn sang her way into his and back into her own body. Each had to take from the other, but then give something back, something precious and lifegiving. Something that initially started with the breath.

In the smoke of forest fires, war, anger, the pandemic, pollution, lies, we have to learn to breathe in kindness and love, even in the face of fear and death. Only by loving death can we become fully entangled in life. This is the cost of all relationships. To dive deeply into the waters of climate change we are asked to do the same. We begin to build a relationship with Earth, in my case, with ice, in yours, whatever calls to you. In this relationship we have to entangle ourselves in the possibility of death. In this crisis, things are changing, dying, drying, rising, melting, nothing will ever be the same, not in our lifetimes, maybe not even for the next seven generations, maybe never. Even without a promise of certainty and maybe even more because of this lack, we need to find new songs, new stories for the uncertainty ahead.

In the untangling of Skeleton Woman, we see the threads of a way forward. The only way to untangle ourselves from the threat of climate chaos, is to look at it in the full light of consciousness and still find kindness, compassion, empathy, and love. Not only for all the things we have and will lose, but also for all the things we take for granted, that are less obvious or ignored. The image of climate for many years has been the single polar bear on a small iceberg, there was even one recently that won the People's Choice award of the 2023 Wildlife Photographer of the Year award from the Natural History Museum, London (2023). Compassion for the bear is valid and hopefully connects many to the plight of these regions of the world, but it downplays the complexity. It does not honor the tangles in the unconscious realms.

Glancing at the beauty and softness of the bear on the ice, the ice is merely a background player, ignored and dismissed. This goes for the water underneath the image and the people in these regions who's lives are disrupted by minimal sea ice and loss of hunting or fishing grounds, those who are forced to make choices to allow drilling in the precious waters as their traditional ways of life are stripped away because of how tangled these regions have become with global warming and the insidious effects of the fossil fuel industry. To sit with the image of the singular polar bear, we have to have patience to untangle it fully. We wait for the realization of all the harms that are interconnected to sing themselves into our consciousness. Drumming the rhythms of truth and love into our very bones. This song of consciousness can only be learned in the waiting. This is what I learned at the bedside of my mother and beside the dying ice.

If we can sit and untangle, looking Lady Death in the face with kindness, we can get to know her and how vitally important she is to the world today. To love death, the death of all the things that no longer serve our health, wellbeing, relationships, Earth, the vulnerable, the forgotten, the ignored, all those who are pushed into the unconscious of our society, only then can we begin to find a rebirth after death. As we begin to "sing the song of consciousness" only then "will we feel the burn of truth, we throw a burst of fire into the darkness of psyche so we can see … what we're truly doing, not what we wish to think we are doing" (Pinkola-Estes, 1997, p. 156). When this happens, the veil is lifted, we are laid bare to one another and to the world. Only from here can a true relationship with what we have done and continue to do be recognized fully, only from here can we begin to imagine a different way forward.

In the tale of Sedna, Skeleton Woman, Lady Death, she is an angokok, a shaman, one who knows the ways of magic, the wyrding ways. She can see beyond the world of the material to the depths of the unconscious. She straddles both realms, entangling everything in her tendrils. The only way to begin to untangle is to move into this realm of time out of time. Time out of time, as in, beyond the confines of time as we know it, like in a dream where a whole life is condensed into a moment. But also, in a time where we realize we are out of time. The time to reverse what we have done, especially those of us who descend from these WEIRD generations of the industrialized West. Especially those in positions of power, or who can speak directly to those in power, through the democratic process, through monied interests, through mass movements, everyone is needed to acknowledge and sing these songs of consciousness.

Consciousness that we have left too many behind, that we have given too much to too few (in the United States, according to the Congressional Budget Office's, 2022 report, as of 2019 the richest one percent of households in the US-owned one-third of the country's wealth, just one more example of our growing wealth and income inequality), and that we find ourselves entangled in a complexity of our own making. In the tale, the fisherman is the one who threw out his net after all! In what seems like a blink of an eye, we have transformed this planet in our image, in the image of fire and industrialization. The ice is melting faster than it ever has before and time is collapsing. We have already lost too much time over the years to inaction and corporate lobbying. We have to untangle ourselves from the net of greed and overshoot. In this untangling we can learn who we are, we can begin to hear the rhythms of the Earth again, to begin to align ourselves to her song, and in doing so, sing both of ourselves back to life.

Once we can see the tangle, the complexity of where we have landed, we need to begin to build. Build a cathedral to the future and memorials to all we have lost. Commemorate not only the good, but also the bad, the history of what got us here, these are their own gifts to the future. If we can acknowledge where we failed, we can learn from these mistakes and move forward. This is the gift of imperfection. Similarly, the gifts of uncertainty are vital to move us into the future. Only by sitting in the dark, facing our fears and past mistakes, can we look on Lady Death with kindness and begin to untangle, dream, weep, have heart, and move forward.

A Seed of Reflection

In each section as death and destruction are explored, I want to acknowledge the life that comes forward as well. I have aspired to find a complex, but hopeful balance throughout. Following the note from the prior chapter on pyrophytes and pyrophiles, the seeds springing from destruction are a beautiful and nuanced metaphor for the necessary path forward. There is a moment of sacrifice, of death, which leads to rebirth. This rebirth can only happen because of that necessary death. In the story of the A23a iceberg, there is a similarly complex note of hope when discussing the imminent, though long, drawn-out death of this giant.

When icebergs, especially like this one, begin to die, to break down and melt in the sea or ocean, those that were land bound or scraping the seafloor become vital nutrients to the ecosystem around them. Given the vastness of A23a and others, they become a whole new ecosystem all to themselves, even creating their own weather above. Underneath though, even as "their destiny is to fragment and wither to nothing. Their legacy is the ocean life they seed by dropping entrained mineral nutrients. From plankton up to great whales—all benefit from the melting bergs' fertilisation effect" (Amos, 2024). In its own way it is a pyrophyte, reseeding after being burned. In the overheating of the climate, it melts and brings new life to all that swim in its wake. The blue bones of this icy giant serve to create a new world, like the bones of Ymir. Bones that, once untangled from all the ills done to them, can grow new flesh and new life.

Take a moment to sit, untangling what has come before. Breathe into that space of not knowing what will come next. Then, dream a dream that tears the world apart and builds her anew, a dream that brings with it tears from the ice and connects you to the world around you. Dive into the waters and envision the bones upon which the whole world grows.

Resources

Amos, J. (2024, January 15). A23a: Spectacular arches, caves as monster iceberg decays. *BBC News*. https://www.bbc.com/news/science-environment-67986443

Astier, H. (2019, April 15). Notre-Dame fire: What the cathedral means to the French. *BBC News*. https://www.bbc.com/news/world-europe-47942786

Congressional Budget Office (2022). *Trends in the distribution of family wealth,* 1989 *to 2019*. https://www.cbo.gov/system/files/2022-09/57598-family-wealth.pdf

Coren, M. J., (2023, December 19). It's time to start planning for the next thousand years: Climate change desperately needs 'cathedral projects' by Washington Post Climate Coach column https://www.washingtonpost.com/climate-environment/2023/12/19/climate-change-cathedral-project/

Douglas, J. (1972). Appendix to opinion of Douglas, J. dissenting: Extract from oral arguments of the solicitor general. From *Sierra Club v. Morton*, 404–405 U.S. 727 (1972). https://supreme.justia.com/cases/federal/us/405/727/

Durham World Heritage Site (Accessed January 5, 2024). *Cathedral building in the middle ages*. Durham Castle and Cathedral UNSCO World Heritage Site. https://www.durhamworldheritagesite.com/learn/architecture/cathedral/construction

Greenfield, P. (2021, December 2). Plans to mine Ecuador forest violate rights of nature, court rules. *The Guardian*. https://www.theguardian.com/environment/2021/dec/02/plan-to-mine-in-ecuador-forest-violate-rights-of-nature-court-rules-aoe

Luckhurst, T. (2019, August 17). Iceland's Okjokull glacier commemorated with plaque. *BBC News*. https://www.bbc.com/news/world-europe-49345912

Magnason, A. S. (2019). *A letter to the future* [public commemorative plaque]. Okjokull glacier, Iceland.

Maisonnave, F., de Miguiel, T., & Penner, A. (2023, August 7). Indigenous leader inspires Amazon city to grant personhood to an endangered river. *Associated Press*. https://apnews.com/article/brazil-amazon-wari-indigenous-nature-rights-deforestation-68af65663fb7bd1b9d2051ce10c17a46

NASA & JPL Caltech (2023, August 23). *Video: Greenland ice mass loss 2002–2023* [Multimedia with video]. Global Climate Change. NASA.

Natural History Museum London (2023). *Ice bed, Nima Sarikhani*. https://www.nhm.ac.uk/wpy/gallery/2023-ice-bed

Perry, N. (2022, August 15). New Zealand River's personhood status offers hope to Māori. *Associated Press.*

Pinkola-Estes, C. (1997). *Women who run with wolves: Myths and stories of the wild woman archetype*. Ballantine Books.

Samuel, S. (2019, August 18). This country gave all its rivers their own legal rights. *Vox.* https://www.vox.com/future-perfect/2019/8/18/20803956/bangladesh-rivers-legal-personhood-rights-nature

Sturluson, S. (2005). *The Prose Edda* [Penguin Classics] (J. Byock, Trans.). Penguin Books.

Surma, K. (2022, May 4). Indian court rules that nature has legal status on par with humans—And that humans are required to protect it. *Inside Climate News.* https://insideclimatenews.org/news/04052022/india-rights-of-nature/

5 Coral, Reflecting in a World of Blood and Bones

The world of coral is a world of bones, of living, colorful, heart wrenchingly beautiful bones. In the mythology of coral, it is also a world drenched in blood. As shown in Norse mythology above, during the creation of the world, Midgard, the oceans were made from the blood of Ymir. In Greek mythology, coral was born of blood. Blood within blood. In the myth of Perseus, the origins of coral are illuminated. Coral can only be born through the spilling of blood, specifically the blood of the Gorgon, Medusa. Mythologically, the Gorgons were three monstrous sisters, of the three, only Medusa could be killed, the other two are immortal. They are described in various ways, most commonly "with hissing serpents instead of hair, boar's tusks instead of teeth, hands of brass and wings of gold" (Chevalier & Gheerbrant, 1996/1969, p. 446) also, often "with bodies covered with golden scales" (Hamilton, 1998/1942, p. 204). They are human, gods, and animals all in one monstrous form, singular and multiple.

Medusa's origin story tells of her transformation and her deep connection to the sea. She was once quite the beauty and the god of the oceans, Poseidon, took her as a lover. One day. "the pair made their bed within a chapel of Athena" (Monaghan, 2000/1981, pp. 212–213). This act so offended Athena, the Goddess of Wisdom, that she made it a mission to ruin Medusa. She transformed her into a Gorgon and eventually paved the way for Perseus to slay her. In other origin stories, the Gorgons are the granddaughters of Gaia, Mother Earth (Campbell, 1976/1964, p. 153) and were thought to represent those earlier Earth-based goddesses that many matriarchal cultures and faiths worshiped long before the Greeks more patriarchal, heroic myths were recorded.

Joseph Campbell (1976/1964), a preeminent writer in comparative mythology, wrote about Medusa briefly in his *Occidental Mythology*. He likens her to those "daemons that formerly had symbolized the force of the cosmic order itself, the dark mystery of time, which licks up hero deeds like dust… ever turning in its circle of eternal return" (p. 24). In this split, the move from these older mythologies to the newer, the striving hero takes the stage, vanquishing that which sprang from the fertile, feminine, soil of Earth itself. This

DOI: 10.4324/9781032644820-6

is the myth that is still playing out in our industrialized and modern era, one which WEIRD cultures embrace thoroughly (Western, educated, industrialized, rich, and democratic societies (Henrich et al, 2010)). This mastery of natural forces and separation of the individual, not only from one another but the planet we are all trying to survive upon but from one another, is where these myths have now outgrown their usefulness.

In this era of ecological crisis, perhaps it is time to return to this mysterious realm of "the cursed yet gravid earth, which, though defeated and subdued, are with their powers never totally absorbed" (Campbell, 1964/1976, p. 25). No matter how much our modern world would like to imagine they are above and beyond the natural world, we are all intimately a part of it. In the myth, clad in a variety of charmed and magical (wyrd, or perhaps WEIRD objects) gifted to him from the gods, Perseus beheads Medusa as she is sleeping. With the strike of his sword, her blood is released. Here, the tale varies. In some, it seems the blood, imbued with Medusa's power to turn anyone who gazed upon her to stone, solidifies, becoming the prized red coral. In others, Perseus sets her head on the shore of a beach as he tends to further questing. The blood leaks into the sea, the red tendrils petrifying into coral branches. In yet another, the touch of the blood on a bed of seaweed and sticks turns them into stoney forms. Whichever origin, coral is born of blood, the blood of an earthly mother goddess.

One cannot take a myth literally, however, there are some interesting reflections of its mythic origin in the natural form of coral. These sea beings are fascinating in their multiplicity just like the Gorgon who birthed them. Corals are animal, vegetable, and mineral. Their base form, the polyp, is similar to a sea anemone. This tissue body can digest and reproduce, they are also responsible for the creation of their calcium-carbonate skeleton. These skeletons are what we call reefs in their largest and most communal form. Within the tissue of many corals, live small algae, *zooxanthellae*, which give them their vibrant color and provide another source of nutrients from photosynthesis. Vegetable, within animal, set atop mineral, all three combine to make the coral we are most familiar with, those that make up large, colorful reefs, such as the Great Barrier Reef in Australia and the like (Figures 6 and 7).

The coral that traces its mythology to Greece is red coral, it is only one of many varieties and is found most commonly in the Mediterranean Sea. "Mediterranean peoples' connection to red coral stretch back to Paleolithic hunter-gatherers" (Spanne, 2021). It is therefore the type the Greeks would have encountered most readily and been fascinated by. Within the cultures who collected it, and given its mythology, it was and is "still believed to have protective and curative powers" (Spanne, 2021). In the myth of Medusa, we are focusing on the goddess in this exploration, so Perseus will be removed for now. Once beheaded, her blood is collected in vials by Asclepius, the God of Healing. The blood was retrieved from her left and right sides, "with the former he slays, but with the latter he cures and brings back to life" (Campbell,

Figure 6 Drawing, *Language of a Reef*, colored pens and markers on paper, by the author.

1964/1976, p. 25). This power of life and death, embedded in the red rings through with echoes from Chapter 3.

The red of coral also brings us into the green of the prior myth, the place of the forest. "Researchers frequently compare red-coral colonies to a forest. Like trees in a forest, the colonies create three-dimensional complexity in the environment, providing shelter and camouflage to other species. Trees affect

Figure 7 Drawing, *Coral Tree Hyperbole,* colored pens and markers on paper, by the author.

wind currents; corals affect ocean currents" (Spanne, 2021). Unfortunately, as the waters warm today, the red coral has become increasingly more like a field than a forest (Bramanti, as cited in Spanne, 2021). With the increasing warming with very little reprieve, the coral do not have time to recover, so they grow smaller and smaller, if they grow at all in the Mediterranean. This is also the case in many other parts of the world. Beginning in 2023, ocean temperatures were so high that scientists had to restructure their scale for the "higher mortality rates and bleaching levels" (Ajasa, 2024).

In recent years, the draw to publicize coral has been centered on bleaching. There have been a number of mass bleaching events from Florida in the United States to Australia. Bleaching is caused by warming ocean waters. When the water gets too warm, the coral animal expels its vegetable symbiote. This is a defense mechanism to preserve what nutrients it can. When the algae are ejected so is the dynamic color it provides. The tissue of coral is generally translucent, so when this colorful coating is removed the white "bones" of the coral are revealed. This is what constitutes bleaching. As the coral is bleached, we are removed from the creative, life-giving blood that brought coral into being and returned to the realm of Skeleton Woman.

The bleached bones of the coral move us into the loss in our world today. This bleached stage "doesn't mean that the coral is dead, but rather that it is more vulnerable and can die" (Ajasa, 2024). If the water stays warm or does not cool for a long enough time to allow some renewal, the coral will die. It connects us to the reality of death, of all that could be lost. Finding ourselves in the place of coral, we see that "we are now faced with the fact, my friends, that tomorrow is today. We are confronted with the fierce urgency of now. In this unfolding conundrum of life and history, there is such a thing as being too late" (King, 1967). Just like the bleaching of the coral

> life often leaves us standing bare, naked, and dejected with a lost opportunity. The tide in the affairs of men … ebbs. We may cry out desperately for time to pause in her passage, but time is adamant to every plea and rushes on
>
> (King, 1967).

We continue to rush forward with our desires for instant gratification, consumption, and consumerism. This way leads to certain death. Instead, we need to find another way, for, "over the bleached bones and jumbled residues of numerous civilizations are written the pathetic words, 'Too late'" (King, 1967).

Let us hope we are not too late. No doubt, the reality is that we are. At least we are too late to return to the ways it has always been. We have to move forward into a new reality with a new view of the world. The bones, the death of an old way, lead to the new. Just like the fingers of Sedna created the sea life and Medusa's blood the coral.

In the myth of Medusa, the only way to look at her without losing oneself was through a reflection. In the myth, the tool used to effectuate this was Athena's aegis, her shield. This shield was polished so brightly that it was like a mirror (Hamilton, 1998/1942, p. 204). Once Medusa was slain, her visage was forever emblazoned on this shield, also worn as a breastplate by Athena (Monaghan, 2000, p, 213). This is the further entanglement of the two goddesses. The only way to address this monstrous complexity is through a reflective shield of wisdom. For many, this is the scientific data, but we know from above what a monster that can be.

Data is knowledge, not wisdom. In this place, wisdom is needed to reflect our situation. For me, that is the place of dreams and myths. In the myths of Medusa and Sedna, when the aspects of earth are unacknowledged and ignored, "the more sternly she is cut down, the more frightening will her Gorgoneum be" (Campbell, 1964/1976, p. 153). Sedna entangles all the ocean when she is antagonized, Medusa turns the world to stone, everything set in motion becomes immovable and inflexible. The more we tear parts of our Earth apart, the harsher the consequences of our heroic WEIRD actions become. Our industrialized, capitalistic, patriarchal, colonial ways no longer serve, we have to look at our reflection as it has become monstrous. Once we can look at all we have done and come to terms with our role in it we gain the wisdom to move forward into the unknown ahead.

This is where a further aspect of Medusa is unveiled. In this form she is "characteristic of the guardian of the other world" (Campbell, 1964/1976, p. 154), a psychopomp on the borderland of the unconscious. Here we are again in the realm of uncertainty. Now that we know what we have done, how our striving, prideful push into the modern industrialized way of life has harmed this planet, we need to dive into the depths of grief this should bring. In these depths we become tangled in Sedna's locks again. Pulled down to the bottom of the warming ocean to confront the bones now bare before us.

Though coral bleaching is a natural process, the intensity, severity, and frequency of these events is growing every year. This is a direct response to the warming of the ocean. The ocean warms as the planet warms. There is no conscious messaging on the part of the coral, it is just what they do in response to their ecological surroundings. However, it does feel like, through the mirror of the mythic, that these beaching incidents could be viewed as an eye-catching cry for help. They are revealing the bones of the issue that stands before us. If we do not find a way to stop the cycle of warming, these brilliant forms will fade. The remnants of oceanic forests burned down in the wildfires of the boiling seas.

In the summer of 2023, António Guterres, secretary general of the United Nations stated, "the era of global warming has ended; the era of global boiling has arrived" (as cited in Bisset, 2023). At that time July had recorded the hottest three days on record and the highest ever ocean temperatures (Bisset, 2023). Though this terminology seems hyperbolic and extreme it can allow us to imagine where the current planetary trends place us if we were coral or ice. The discomfort of it would feel like boiling, indeed, for many, the hotter and more humid summers are placing humanity in a boiling state as well. This use of hyperbole is meant to catch our attention, just like the bleaching coral.

In a fascinating "craft-science collaborative artwork," the Crochet Coral Reef, the hyperbolic nature of coral can be seen through artistic expression (cited in Roberts, 2024). In the oceans, many coral formations are curved in such a way that they "thrive on hyperbolism, so to speak; the curvy structure of coral maximizes nutrient intake" (Roberts, 2024). This wavy structure is celebrated in these fiber-arts exhibits around the world. Each coral is created by a crocheter and then they come together to form these artificial reefs, placed on display "sometimes described as the environmental version of the AIDS quilt" (Roberts, 2024). The technique of crocheting leans into the curvature and unique patterns of these beings, into the hyperbolic. Though the literary and mathematic terms are not identical, as in a dream or myth terms can lean into multiple meanings.

This conflation, or relation, of terms is a fun and enlightening exercise. It allows us to lean into the multiplicity of the space we find ourselves in, one of the hyperobject of global warming and in a place where terminology needs overlap within disciplines. Transdisciplinary, again, has a significant role here, from the mythological, to the mathematical, the complexity of climate is reflected in coral from the curvature of its large form to the necessary collaboration of the minute polyps. Like the communal effort of the crochet project, coral relies on the power of community. "We see mighty coral reefs rising from the depths of the ocean … yet each individual depositor is puny, weak … but their number is their strength" (Jones as cited in Marx and Engels, 1889). Complexity, creativity, and community, all necessary to address the problems we face.

If we cannot lean into the complexity of the challenges ahead, we will be petrified by them, like looking at Medusa head on; striped down to the bone, staring at the stark reality before us. Coral can only thrive when it pulls all of its pieces together. All the contrasting areas that make up coral are symbiotic and relational; despite their differences they unfold into a greater whole. The reefs they create could also be imagined as a sort of cathedral of the sea. If we lose the majority of them and have to "reforest" the oceans, this too would be a cathedral project, one that requires long-term planning and a commons of labor. The tiny polyps demonstrate this commons, a coming together for the greater good.

In the project ahead, we need a project of the commons under the aegis of government to address climate crisis. A coral complexity is required ahead, one that is on the level of the individual, local, and global community, one that embraces the animal, vegetable, and mineral aspects of the world. One cannot go forward without the other, if one piece is left behind or undernourished, the whole will fall. We each need to embrace the commons of the world, the pieces we all share. Not only do we need to embrace them, but we also need to protect and honor them. This is best done by policy at a worldwide level, short of that, nationally or locally. Oceans, rivers, our atmosphere, all these and more are shared resources that we owe to ourselves, each other, and the future generations to protect and preserve.

Policy and constitutional amendments are democratic paths to preserving commons. Legal moves like rights of nature are another process that can be utilized. But the truth of all of these is that they need an upswell of support from the majority of votes, voices, and ventures to make them a reality. To gain popular support, a cultural move is necessary. This is where the final aspect of Medusa and her entanglement with Athena comes into play, that of the arts. Just like the crocheted coral mentioned above, the creative is where change begins to happen. It is also interesting to note that this creative impulse is largely by women, fiber arts were "advanced mostly by women" and in this instance, they have taken a further move to democratize it (Roberts, 2024).

Once Medusa is felled, she gives birth. From her neck her child Pegasus is born from her time with Poseidon. Pegasus is the winged horse of Greek mythology. As Pegasus sprang to life, its "hoof struck Mt. Helicon and caused the fountain Hippocrene (Horse's Fountain) to gush forth, which from then on was loved by the Muses and associated with poetic inspiration" (Morford & Lenardon, 1999, p. 410). Pegasus is forever linked to creative inspiration and by the story of his origin, so is Medusa. Furthermore, Athena invented the flute "in imitation of the Gorgon's lament for Medusa" (Morford & Lenardon, 1999, p. 410). The inspiration from coral is tied not only to creativity but also to sorrow and loss, the loss of Medusa, the Earth Mother. So, coral is also crying out to us, singing a song of lament, a song to open hearts, a song to return us to older ways and wisdom.

We only lament because we love, we mourn because we care. Through the arts, even if one has never felt the plight of the changing climate or Earth's warming, a deeper level of understanding can spring into life. With every blow the earth suffers, the greater the cries to hear the necessary lament. Creative expression can sing us back into a relationship with the world around us, connecting us with the wisdom we need, with the time and space to mourn in community, and with a reflective aegis, the necessary backing, to move forward.

Resources

Ajasa, A. (2024, February 14). Coral bleaching is now so extreme, scientists had to expand their scale for it. *The Washington Post*. https://www.washingtonpost.com/weather/2024/02/14/coral-bleaching-alerts-ocean-warmth/

Bisset, V. (2023, July 29). The U.N. warns 'an era of global boiling' has started. What does that mean? *The Washington Post*. https://www.washingtonpost.com/climate-environment/2023/07/29/un-what-is-global-boiling/

Campbell, J. (1976). *Occidental mythology*. Penguin Press. (Original work published 1964.)

Chevalier, J., & Gheerbrant, A. (1996). *Dictionary of Symbols* (J. Buchanan-Brown, Trans). Penguin Books. (Original work published 1969.)

Hamilton, E. (1998). *Mythology*. Black Bay Books. (Original work published 1942.)

Henrich, J., Heine, S., & Norenzayan, A. (2010). The weirdest people in the world? In *Behavioural and Brain Sciences 33*(2/3) (pp. 61–83).

King, M. L. (1967). *Beyond Vietnam: A time to break silence* [Talk]. https://www2.hawaii.edu/~freeman/courses/phil100/17.%20MLK%20Beyond%20Vietnam.pdf

Marx, K., & Engels, F., (Ed). (1889). *Capital: A critical analysis of capitalist production* (S. Moore & E. Aveling, Trans.). Appleton & Co. https://www.google.com/books/edition/Capital/JyIiAQAAIAAJ?hl=en&gbpv=1

Monaghan, P. (2000). Medusa. In *The new book of goddesses and heroines* (pp. 212–213). Llewellyn Press. (Original work published 1981.)

Morford, M. P., & Lenardon, R. J. (1999). *Classical mythology (Sixth Ed.)*. Oxford University Press.

Roberts, S. (2024, January 15). The crochet coral reef keeps spawning, hyperbolically. *The New York Times*. https://www.nytimes.com/2024/01/15/science/mathematics-crochet-coral.html

Spanne, A. (2021, February 24). The mediterranean's red gold is running out. *The Atlantic*. https://www.theatlantic.com/science/archive/2021/02/red-coral-mediterranean-fishing-climate-change/618124/

Conclusion

Buoying One Another, Connecting Across Rising Tides

Boundaries

There is an interesting anecdote that I found online while researching coral. It is a translation of a tale titled "Wakatobi Sea Ghosts" (Darmawan, 2014) I cannot speak to its authenticity, but it set my imagination alight and I hope it may do the same for you. In this story, set on the ocean around Wakatobi, in the southeast Sulawesi province of Indonesia, a local skipper arrives to take a group out. The author notes that this skipper is renowned and from the Bajo Mola tribe who were once nomadic, living only in boats and who now have houses built on stilts in the water. It is noted that they still honor many ancient traditions and superstitions, they even have rituals to make offerings to the ocean to appease her when needed.

One day, the author of this tale says, they take the opportunity to go out into the ocean on a boat with this skipper. Despite the urging of a crew member, he refuses to take them on a shortcut to their destination. He tells them that "catastrophe would come if we disturbed the occupants here" (Darmawan, 2014 as translated in Indomyths, 2017). Somewhat amused, this passenger relays their experience to a researcher friend. Upon hearing the tale, the researcher smiles and pulls out some maps, asking to see where these ghosts or demons were located. To their surprise, wherever the cursed places were located "there are also barrier reefs, the largest coral gardens, the sinkers of ships" (Darmawan, 2014 as translated in Indomyths, 2017). The author became enamored, musing on these lost ways. The skipper navigated with no modern instruments, with only inherited knowledge he knew where to avoid and how to approach the many hidden dangers of the ocean.

Hidden in the myths and superstitions were conservation techniques as well, they were never to eat the small fish or to litter in the ocean. In these seemingly irrational ways, they had "a guide for protecting and conserving the environment" (Darmawan, 2014 as translated in Indomyths, 2017). The Bajo Mola live as a partner to the ocean, understanding her ways and respecting her needs. This is true of many Indigenous groups in their relationship to the natural world, of which we are all a part. In their careful consideration of these natural boundaries and unseen forces, they not only protect themselves,

DOI: 10.4324/9781032644820-7

but the ecosystem they are embedded and entangled with. Again, I do not know the truth of any of this, that is the way with a folktale, even a more modern one. However, I believe the underlying message is an important piece and holds a truth outside what data and charts can tell us. This is the area of uncertainty that leads to possibilities.

These imaginary boundaries do not cut these cultures off from nature, rather they allow them to coexist in a reciprocal manner. In our modern world, things like buoys are set upon the ocean to mark these imaginaries that we might no longer remember or honor. In their own symbolic way, a buoy is but one point on a boundary, and yet it points toward the whole. Either that whole is submerged, like a hidden reef or shoal, or the whole may be a border or edge of territorial boundaries. Boundaries and borders today take many forms, and we should take care to honor the ghosts that lie within, the forgotten and the dismissed, the unconscious and repressed. Unfortunately, today, many boundaries are not so imaginary, they are harsh borders with even harder messages.

Borders

When I originally heard the chants broadcast on the news of "Build that Wall" at the presidential rallies in the build up to the 2016 campaign, my mind would always wander. This image of a wall seemed to take a hold of me. At first, most likely because it was featured in a show that I was trying to get caught up on, the image of a giant wall of ice from *Game of Thrones* (Martin, 2013) kept coming to mind. This vast, impenetrable barrier, miles high, that spanned from coast to coast, this is what my imagination conjured. But in many ways, I think that was not far off from what was being promised and subsequently built, construction which continues to this day. The plan was a great wall that no one could scale, break, or otherwise penetrate. In the campaign messaging at the time, the wall was one that would somehow spring forward, fully formed, for which no one on this side of it had to pay. It was as much a fantasy at the time as the wall in Westeros (the kingdom where the Game of Thrones book/TV series are set).

As time has passed there have been TV news story after print news article after the tweet, bragging about the choice of wall material, the length of wall that is under construction, and the like. The wall seems to be a settled fact at this point. At the same time, this image of an impenetrable, unscalable wall has found its way, away from the southern border of the United States, and has taken root in our society. Given my fascination with the depths of the unconscious, I pay attention to images repeating the way meteorologists watch weather patterns. When the chants of "build that wall" began to echo, I knew that this image held a potency that could not be fully understood at face value. There had to be something more to it. Of course, there have been others over the years who have taken to using the phrase "build bridges, not walls" as a rallying cry against the xenophobia and racism to which this behemoth at the southern border pointed. This meaning quickly moved into the collective consciousness, but what of the unconscious aspects?

As I've watched the news over the past years, I've seen wall after wall forming. Not walls of ice or fantasy, but literal walls going up around the Capitol and the White House after January 6, 2021, and figurative walls being built throughout the society from time immemorial, but over the past decade especially. For whatever reason, the "unscalable fencing" around our nation's Capital after the pre-inaugural unrest struck me particularly hard. Back in the summer of the prior year, I was living in Washington, DC. I loved to walk through the streets and see the various monuments and national landmarks. When the fencing went up around the White House, it made me sad to some extent, but I'd felt for some time that "The People's House" had been removed from the people. As a regular citizen, I have never been able to get a White House tour (though I know many can) and I have never set foot any closer than whatever barrier was up that day. It is not as inviting or public a space as Capitol Hill in my experience.

As I was working on my dissertation, I was lucky enough to hop on the metro at least a few times a week to do research at the Library of Congress. The whole Capitol complex felt like home to me, it offered a sense that the government was not so far removed as we might think it to be. The House and the Senate seemed to me, walking by those marble facades, more accessible, more attainable, more connected to the people (no matter how idealistic or naïve that may be). After the events of January 6, seeing these fences, these barriers, these walls around the Capitol took hold of me. This image of the wall rooted itself in my consciousness and would not let go. It seemed to haunt me. Besides a casual mention here and there, it seemed this was not such a distraction for others, but it would not let me go and then there was a headline that the President was headed to the border to celebrate the construction of his border wall, and the connections came full circle.

Just as one may wake with a dream and wonder what it might tell about the days to come or what wisdom it is passing on from past experiences, this image of the wall had something more to tell me, something I was missing because of its obviousness. In *Game of Thrones* (Martin, 2013), the ice wall is an ancient structure. Barely anyone remembers how it came to be or why it is there. Much like the haunted ocean of Indonesia mentioned earlier, there is some wisdom hiding within that needs to be honored, even if it cannot be understood fully. This icy boundary divides the kingdoms below the wall, from the wilds above. There is something foreboding and comforting in it, this frozen surface that holds fast forever. The bright white ice looks like marble in its solid perfection. It is a structure that can withstand anything. This fantasy wall is far from the dark slatted fencing on the border, but the tension of separation versus safety that it symbolizes is the same.

The ice wall of *Game of Thrones* (Martin, 2013) protects as much as it divides, this is the argument for the border wall and that fencing around the Capitol. We can build walls forever protecting ourselves, but we will always be divided by them. The figurative walls that hateful rhetoric built are, much like the border walls that are under construction on our border with Mexico, just an addition to the walls that were already there. We have had walls in our society separating and protecting us for as long as the ice wall of Westeros: racism, classism, xenophobia, homophobia, misogyny, ableism, and others. Most people have lived so long with their walls they don't know how to function without them, the idea that these barriers are under threat is a dire concern. For others, these walls serve only to divide, they remove protections that others have access to because of how or where the walls are built. This is the problem with a wall. It cannot protect without separating.

Even without the unscalable fencing around the Capitol, my idealistic view of those marble facades, are to others, unscalable walls. The journey to reach the ear of a government official seems as daunting as scaling miles of vertical ice or crossing an ocean with shipwrecking reefs. This is not what we want for our government. This is not what we need as a society. We cannot continue to build walls between one another, no matter how safe they make us feel.

The bridge is perhaps a helpful and comforting symbol to some. As an antidote to the wall, it seems useful, but within it, underneath it, there is still a divide, a loss or lack. On each side of the bridge there is uneven terrain and underneath it a deadly drop. Therefore, I offer the remains of the Berlin Wall as restorative symbol for our divided nation. In this image there is not only a recognition of our past, but it also puts us all on similar footing, in the same landscape. What is left of the Berlin Wall has been endlessly tagged and scarred by the citizenry, by artists, by activists. It has transformed not only in physical form but symbolically as well. This is what we need our walls to become, monuments that lament our past and give us a creative view forward.

We need to tear down our walls and form them anew. They need to be graffitied and crumbling so that the landscapes on either side can be seen by those who were once divided. There will always be walls, they serve a purpose, but the more daunting walls within us need to dissolve, to become overgrown and obsolete. The walls that I named above, that this current era has served to expand upon for some and to begin a process of dissolution for others, need to be scaled so that we can reach those on the other side. Better yet, they need to break away, be broken down and turned into something new to commemorate the losses endured and remember the lessons that were so hard earned.

Jung wrote "that when an inner situation is not made conscious, it happens outside as fate" and furthermore, if this move to consciousness is not made "the world must perforce act out the conflict and be torn into opposing halves" (Jung, 1951/1979, p. 71). Until we as a society (I speak as an American to my own country, but this is certainly the case in many other parts of the world was well) recognize the more abstract things that divide us, no matter the protection they promise, these walls keep us from understanding and we will continue to see physical walls constructed. The longer a wall stands, the more likely we are to believe it should continue to be there. The fencing that was around the Capitol for safety remained up for longer than the original promise of a month, but it did finally come down. I imagine it is tucked away in some storage building on the outskirts of Washington, DC, just biding its time until it is put to use again. If it had not been removed, depending on how long it stayed up, we may not remember a time it was not there, certainly this is the case in many stretches of our southern border. This may seem like hyperbole, yes, but there are many walls we live with now that we do not need, however, we cannot remember a time when they were ever absent.

Once walls become the norm, they become a part of the permanent landscape, we even cease to see them in some cases. We forget how they got there and assume they just always existed. The thing about an old wall is it's easier to scale or tear down once we recognize it is there. The surface erodes, pock marks make good fingerholds, concrete chips, metal rusts, the structural integrity diminishing with every passing day. Nature has a way. Walls are worn down by water and time, overgrown by greenery. Therefore, the trick is finding the walls that are there, the ones that no longer serve: the ones that are so faded and rusted they are camouflaged, the newer ones that we readily see, but know we can do without, and those that we prefer weren't built in the first place because we saw the divide they caused.

Let's start to tear down those walls in our hearts and minds. Let's start chipping away at them. Let's break them apart until only pieces remain, to create a path forward on equal footing. On the remnants, let vines grow and graffiti build up, paint messages of remembrance and hope for new generations to give them an open path forward. Remind them that there were walls here that no longer serve; that the walls we build in ourselves can only serve to supplement walls already out in the world; remind us that a wall is never just a wall, it can never serve only one purpose, to protect, it must divide. The next time you see a wall, I hope you will view it with new eyes. I hope it will serve as a reminder to examine the walls within to prevent the need to build more walls out in the world. We need to reimagine these walls as porous boundaries, imaginary spaces where we become uncertain. Imagine them as places like the ghostly realms of those coral laden waters, as places where a buoy is sufficient, only there to remind us of our connection and to uplift others.

Buoys

The work of Pauline Boss and Joanna Macy are both wonderful buoys for grief and loss, both ambiguous and otherwise, personally and in relation to climate chaos. Boss (1999), in her work with ambiguous loss, noted that those she works with are "able to find meaning in the midst of ambiguity because of their ability to remain optimistic, creative, and flexible" (p. 132). In Boss' work with these areas of uncertainty, an ability to reframe the loss or to make greater meaning out of it is a balm to the wound. In Macy's writing (Macy & Johnstone, 2012), she looks to the specifics of climate and gives equally creative, optimistic, and flexible solutions to addressing the grief and loss in this topic. She mentions taking a different view, one that she relates to what she calls The Great Turning. In this move we begin to "make friends with uncertainty" and in this turning "we can become strengthened by the gifts it has to offer" (p. 230). This is a lot of what we have been moving toward.

Marris (1996) reminds us that "uncertainty is a fundamental condition of human life" (p. 1) and "reciprocal, co-operative strategies" are key (p. 5). A life buoy is the image I want to call up here, like a large orange donut thrown into uncertain waters. This buoy can remind us of our connection in its circular nature. It is also a type of mandala. Mandalas are an archetype of wholeness, one that Jung wrote is a "uniting symbol," one that expresses "completeness and union" (1954/1975, p. 79). In her *Doughnut Economics*, Kate Raworth (2017) wrote that this area of the doughnut, in terms of a circular vision of the economy, is the goldilocks zone. When we go outside the outer edge we are pushing the boundaries of our planetary ecology, when we break the inner circle we dip into areas of "critical human deprivation" (p. 9). We have to stay within the donut, the buoy, the mandala, to find a whole, equitable, just way forward.

Jung (1954/1975) also noted that the mandala is deeply tied to dreams and is "a natural symbol" that functions as a type of mediation (p. 90) pulling opposites together. Bobbing between the push and pull of the tides of uncertainty, the buoy of the dream and the natural wyrding ways of the dream save us from ourselves. In this place, we are in the middling again, in the not knowing, in the mystery of what is ahead. The doughnut economics that Raworth (2017) suggests is a collection of suggestions which she meant for others to build upon. It is a thought buoy, one that places Earth and compassion for others at the fore. In Chapter 2 above, *Earth for All* (Dixson-Decleve et al, 2022) seems to be building on a lot of her ideas, even the symbolism presented is donut-like, a mandala for a conscious path forward. In this circular reasoning we can envision and imagine a complex and concerned politics to address what the twenty-first century has to hold. One that has big ideas for big problems, one that has layers and levels to address the extreme complexity we face. One that does not dismiss all that we do not know, but leaves a possibility, a donut hole open for all we may discover or that we may never anticipate, for uncertainty.

The beauty and gift of uncertainty as I see it, and as I hope has been expressed in the prior chapters, is that there is possibility in not knowing. There is a way forward in the both/and that leaves us open to mystery and unknown treasure. What I have hoped to lean into as well is, less an active hope, in

Macy's terminology, but more a complex hope. For those of us who do not see ourselves as activists what we do to confront climate change can be especially daunting. It is complex and nuanced. There is always the possibility of going out into the world to march and protest with others, this is an active hope. However, there is a more complex hope that also moves us inward. This is one where we fall in love with Earth, honoring the loss that brings. This is what I hope, yes, hope, to imbue here. To find an image of Earth that means the world to you.

We each need our own story to tell in these times of uncertainty. These stories need to be complex, they need to embrace the grief, become entangled in the loss, sacrifice willingly the things that no longer serve, find creative and protective ways forward, and to transgress boundaries to connect with all that is overlooked. Only by loving all that we will, are, and have lost can these stories come to life in each of us. For me, ice was the way in, for others perhaps it will be the forests, seeds, coral … which one speaks to you? Which one is calling out from beyond the boundaries we set for ourselves? Is there a myth or story you already love that can be amplified and connected to our current crisis? Whatever that looks like for you, become entangled in it and feel it. Dream and sing it into your flesh, down into your bones.

Perhaps in this singing your voice will join with others, maybe you will be inspired to join a march or protest, maybe you will find an active expression of your complex hope. At the same time, and just as importantly, in whatever you already do, bring this new story, this image that is alive in you now, into relationship. Once you become comfortable with them, you can introduce them to others. A recent study shows that there are many more people who support climate policy than we typically think, in fact, we greatly underestimate how many people think these policies are worthwhile (Sparkman et al., 2022, p. 1). Americans estimate that, at most, 43% agree that mitigation is needed, however, the reality is 66–80% (Sparkman et al., 2022, p. 1).

So, take your story and share it. If you are an academic, use this in your teaching and writing, let your students or colleagues see your new companion, and help others to love them too. If you are a therapist or analyst, help your clients or analysands when they encounter these images of loss and uncertainty. Take your experience of loving amid the loss and when you see it reflected in them, hold that space, allow the image to speak and the relationship to grow. Whatever you do, whatever image, myth, or story calls out to you, find your place within it and share the love you find there.

Even in the most terrible nightmares there is an essence of healing and wholeness, this is what I was taught early on in my study of dreams. This is what I have learned in my deep relationship with the ice. Even in the darkest moments, when the doom and gloom are overwhelming and all seems lost, I can imagine into that place with ice and find the beauty in our wounded world. Like the fisherman who can look with kindness on Sedna in her skeletal form or Gawain heading into the deep green of the wood, relationships made in these places of uncertainty change us and our view of the world, our understanding of what we have always known to be true. To enter into relationship with Earth, to dive into these unconscious realms of the image, demands a new way of relating. It involves waiting, not knowing, and a wyrding way of mystery.

The myths that we have explored here "continue to rest in the dark presences … a residue of mystery remains to them … as though speaking silently, to say, 'But do you not hear the deeper song?'" (Campbell, 1964/1976, p. 25). This song, one of lament and memory is what will carry us forward into a renewed vision of the future, full of uncertainty and possibility, into places of connection and creativity. In this place we know that we have lost too much already and that there is still more to lose, but here, we find a north star of an image to guide us, a companion on this journey, one that moves us from the WEIRD ways to the wyrd, into the mystery and the magic of the natural world. In this place we know that we are not separate from the crisis we are entangled in, but deeply intertwined. Every aspect of what we do must reimagine itself in this new reality: our politics, our economics, our creativity, our culture, our psychology, our relationships, our grief, and our hope.

Resources

Boss, P. (1999). *Ambiguous loss: learning to live with unresolved grief.* Harvard University Press.

Campbell, J. (1976). *Occidental mythology.* Penguin Press. (Original work published 1964.)

Darmawan, Y. (2014, January 5). *Hantu-hantu laut di Wakatobi.* https://www.timur-angin.com/2014/01/hantu-hantu-laut-di-wakatobi.html?m=1

Dixson-Decleve, S., Gaffney, O., Ghosh, J., Randers, J., Rockstrom, J., & Stoknes, P.E. (2022). *Earth for all: A survival guide for humanity.* New Society Publishers.

Jung, C. G. (1975). Psychology and religion (R. F. C. Hull, Trans.). In H. Read et al. (Series Eds.), *The collected works of C.G. Jung* (vol. 11, pp. 3–106). Princeton University Press. (Original work published 1954.)

Jung, C. G. (1979). Aion (R. F. C. Hull, Trans.). In H. Read et al. (Series Eds.), *The collected works of C.G. Jung* (vol. 9ii). Princeton University Press. (Original work published 1951.)

Macy, J., & Johnstone, C. (2012). *Active hope: How to face the mess we're in without going crazy.* New World Library.

Marris, P. (1996). *Politics of uncertainty: Attachment in private and public life.* Routledge.

Martin, G. R. (2013). *A song of ice and fire (vol. 1–5).* Bantam Books.

Raworth, K. (2017). *Doughnut economics: Seven ways to think like a 21st-century economist.* Chelsea Green Publishing.

Sparkman, G., Geiger, N., & Weber, E. U. (2022). Americans experience a false social reality by underestimating popular climate policy support by nearly half. In *Nature Communications, 13*(4779) (pp. 1–9). https://www.nature.com/articles/s41467-022-32412-y

Wakatobi sea ghosts. (2017, August 30). Indomyths. https://indomyths.wordpress.com/2017/08/30/sulawesi-sea-ghosts/

Epilogue

In the spirit of creativity and wonder, I have included a handful of images throughout this text which helped me process and imagine a way forward as I was researching and writing. This was done in my own nascent version of Jungian arts-based research inspired by Susan Rowland and Joel Weishaus (2021). When I was laying out the chapter titles, I wanted them to provoke emotion and be symbolic in the way lines of a poem would be. Once they were all in place and I felt they were representative of each section, I began adding them together in a play on a pantoum poem. I would like to share that here as a final note of wyrd, an antidote to the long prose above and a pause before the reader moves on. A moment of wonder as you wander forward, onto your own path in these ever-changing climates.

Climates of Uncertainty, Ambiguity, and Loss

Navigating doom into an uncertain future,
entangled in viscous tides.
Shadows of green shroud fires of change,
tears from the melting ice.
Entangled in viscous tides,
coral, reflecting. In a world of blood and bones,
tears from the melting ice
buoy one another, connecting across rising tides.
Coral, reflecting in a world of blood and bones,
shadows of green shroud fires of change.
Buoying one another, connecting across rising tides,
navigating doom into an uncertain future.

Resource

Rowland, S., & Weishaus, J. (2021). *Jungian arts-based research and "The nuclear enchantment of New Mexico"*. Routledge.

DOI: 10.4324/9781032644820-8

Index

Note: *Italic* page numbers refer to figures.

For Product Safety Concerns and Information please contact our EU representative GPSR@taylorandfrancis.com
Taylor & Francis Verlag GmbH, Kaufingerstraße 24, 80331 München, Germany

www.ingramcontent.com/pod-product-compliance
Lightning Source LLC
LaVergne TN
LVHW010938110826
845149LV00013B/2658

* 9 7 8 1 0 3 2 6 4 4 8 3 7 *